ESCAPE THE CUBICLE

By Joe Shaughnessy

Joe Shaughnessy

Printed in the United States of America

First Printing, 2019

ISBN: 9781099137747 (Print)
ASIN: B07RYW5WPF

www.joeshaughnessy.com

ALSO BY JOE SHAUGHNESSY

Escape the Cubicle

For Younger Readers

Orion's War

Lilly and the Forbidden Forest

Joe Shaughnessy

Table of Contents

Part 2 - Life

Joe Shaughnessy

For Dad

INTRODUCTION

I wrote this book with a specific person in mind. That person has hopes, dreams, and ideas, but they are too afraid to change.

They are too afraid to try new things, or to fail, or to look stupid in front of their peers.

They are stuck — wondering why they constantly fail, while others are getting ahead.

—

The person I'm writing to is fictitious — they don't actually exist. I came up with this idea of a person who was stuck in a job or sitting in a cubicle all day hating their life.

However, as I wrote the content for this piece, I realized that person was you. That person was me.

I began to see the truth in every story. There are lots of hurting people out there, just trying to get by, and achieve the next thing.

Everyone thinks they're miserable, or making mistakes, or somehow got the short-stick in life.

Everyone is stuck.

—

The goal of these stories is simple. It's to show that failing is ok.

It's ok to take risks and pursue ideas. It's ok to look stupid and to get a little mud on your face. Because when you come out the other side in life, you will be that much stronger and wiser.

You will have grown.

—

This book is a collection of essays and ideas — concepts to challenge your thought process. These stories are the inspiration I have followed in order to accomplish my own goals in life.

I hope you can see the theme, that everyone starts with nothing. That people who are pursuing wild dreams, were in fact, the same miserable people like you, staring at cubicle walls, wondering how to escape.

I hope you can learn something from these ideas and apply it to your own life.

I hope you can face failure head-on, and instead, choose to be brave.

Part 1 - Work

FOLLOWING DREAMS

Listen, I'm the last person you should ask on how to follow dreams. I feel like I've been doing that my whole life, and failing exceptionally along the way.

Let's see – where to begin...

There was the time I wanted to be a professional soccer player. Then open an internet t-shirt shop. Be a radio DJ. Be a computer programmer. Make computer games. Be a database designer. A retail manager. Be a restaurant server and live vicariously along the beach. Be a video game tester. Make websites. Sell websites. Be a stand-up comedian. Be a financial advisor. Be a corporate ladder climber. Be a teacher. Be a writer. Be an internet start-up founder. Be a marketer. Tell stories. Work at home. Be a career coach.

The trouble is, these weren't pipe dreams or fantasies – these were things I actually pursued as a passion.

So how does all that experience culminate in who I am today?

The answer, generally, is, I have no idea.

As I pursued each "dream," I would slam into an impenetrable crossroads – something so intrinsically difficult and frustrating to cause me to quit. Often times it was a mental hang-up, the feeling of a vice grip on my brain, telling me I couldn't put up with the torture anymore.

So I quit. And I quit a lot.

The problem with quitting is the pain never subsides. It never actually gets easier to quit anything.

It's like you signed up for a good idea, which at the time sounded terrific, but after spending a year doing it, you suddenly realize it's not a good fit anymore – that you can't possibly see a good outcome even years down the road.

But for anyone on the outside – no one cares that you quit. It's only an internal struggle, that you have to admit the initial idea wasn't solid, and you made a mistake – it's the "admittance of the mistake" that hurts the most.

But for the pain – yeah – that never goes away.

What all that quitting does though, is make you wiser.

Before you start that "next big idea," you're able to culminate all the past lessons in your mind.

You're able to figure out potential hiccups and speed bumps down the road.

Suddenly you're a bigger, better, stronger version of yourself.

What 25-year-old you could only fantasize about knowing, reality-you of a 35-year-old, has 10 years of mistakes and life lessons under his belt. He's able to articulate, "If I sign up for 'X' for the next couple of years, what would that look and feel like, and can I navigate any trouble along the way?"

If you can see already, the 25-year-old is an optimistic moron. He knows nothing. He has no life experience.

The 35-year-old then isn't without fault, he's pessimistic at best. But he's able to shoot down pipe dream ideas, knowing they won't work because of X, Y, and Z.

For example, I wanted to open a donut food truck. I love donuts, and food trucks are trendy, so obviously that would be a smashing success. I also know a delicious donut when I eat one.

The 25-year-old me would open the food truck, like a moron, and fail miserably in a flame of horror. I wouldn't have seen the trouble to come down the road, the difficult and frustrating issues that would drive me crazy and make me quit.

But the 35-year-old me, looks at the food truck and thinks: How would I feel about working nights and weekends (because that's always a soul-crusher)? Where am I getting funding for this operation? How would I continue to make money, and sales questions, and marketing questions? How do I feel about managing difficult employees, or customers? Will I ever have free time, or time with my family?

In what creative ways will this food truck turn into a personal torture device?

What other things are going to cause me to fail? How can I avoid failure at all cost?

Then 35-year-old me will look at statistics and past mistake of other food trucks. Why are they going out of business? What are the successful ones doing? Why are restaurants in general a bad investment?

It's like a paranoid brainstorm of why this business might crush my soul.

—

Where am I going with all this?

I sound like the biggest dream killer in the world – but that couldn't be further from the truth.

I'm a huge proponent of following your dreams – I've been doing it my entire life. I get so fed up with a current situation and desperately want to pursue something new or anything else that provides meaning in my life.

And then I go for it.

You should too.

But here's what going to happen along the way – you're going to fail.

Also know this: Failing is ok.

No one cares that you failed. The only person who's truly affected by the failure is yourself. You're the only one who's going to beat yourself up for failure.

You just have to be ok with that.

—

I know this: 10 years of failure, and trying new things, molds you into a different person.

Spend 10 years trying new things, chasing after dreams, and risk looking stupid in front of your peers.

You can't be afraid of other people – because all they're ever going to do is squawk along the sideline – while you'll be hustling and growing before their eyes.

Because crazy things happen when you take big risks. You learn a lot about yourself for sure, but also new opportunities open before you that you would never see before.

And wild things happen when you're generous, compassionate, and try to help people. Go down the rabbit hole of helping people, and an entire world of possibilities will open before you, that was previously closed to the younger you.

I can promise this: It will be hard. And it will be frustrating.

But at the end of the day, you'll be a better person for it.

A wiser person – with better ideas, stronger ideas, and more life-changing ideas.

Just go for it. It'll be ok.

WORK IS PRISON

Work is a prison.

The cubicle is your cell.

It's like we've all been "sentenced to work." We're on this strange "work-release" program, where we log 40 hours a week into a prison sentence, but then are on probation each evening and every weekend.

—

Imagine this illustration wasn't such a fabrication.

Imagine you literally woke up early each morning, to a blaring alarm clock, and the first thought you have stepping out of bed is: "Crap. I have to go to prison today."

As you enter the shower, your mind swirls with the misery that will entail – the horrible prison guards, the self-absorbed warden, the annoying cellmates, the riots, the impossible boredom, and the meaningless tasks.

Can you really live through another day of 8 hours with nothing to do? Or stamping another repetitive license plate? Or picking up another soda bottle as motorists speed by?

You figure you can take the abuse – you have to, after all – there are bills to pay.

—

I don't see much difference between the two, work and prison.

While at work, all our liberties are stripped away. We're forced to work on tasks we care nothing about. All we ever hope for is some relief, that there will be downtime, or articles to read, or the internet to browse. And low-and-behold, when our boss is out of the office, it feels like a regular holiday at work – a true reason to rejoice.

—

I read recently 85% of people are "disconnected" at work. That means they're coasting by, just collecting a paycheck, or are so "actively disengaged" that they're applying for other jobs or consciously harming the company they work for.

That number – 85% – may astound you. But for any corporate drone, stuck working for Corporate America, they'll see that number and understand the truth: the number is glaringly accurate.

No one is working.

Granted, there are pockets of success globally. The United States, as it happens, has more "millennial-friendly" companies who are enticing workers with better benefits, like remote working and flexible workplaces. Only 70% of US workers are disengaged.

But consider how Western Europe fares, as 90% of the workers are disengaged. Wow. If you've been unlucky enough to interact with a European company, you understand this fact. For one, it feels like the entire summer is off the table – don't bother talking to them during their 7 weeks of guaranteed vacation – I'm looking at you France.

But let's not pick on one specific country or time-off standards – after all, we should all be "free" and have unlimited vacations if we please. I'm not convinced the American corporate (prison) system with its measly 2 vacation weeks is any better.

But what Europeans do – and they know exactly what they're doing – is they "pretend to work." They attend useless meetings and delay projects for an ungodly amount of time – just to save face and pretend like they have work to do. They're saving their jobs, creating meaningless busy-work, just for a paycheck at a job they hate.

Is that a great way to live?

—

Most important to the success of the Americans – to the 30% of workers who are "engaged and happy at work" – is tapping into each worker's unique talents – it's really that simple of a fix.

If I desperately want to be a writer, for example, then why am I forced to talk on the phone, or deal with angry customers, or do graphic design projects?

Obviously, that's an easy fix: Give me writing projects to do.

But that's not how Corporate America works, at least on the whole.

We have arcane leadership systems, with managers plucked from the marine corps, who drill us with instructions in loud booming voices, and expect results yesterday.

Work harder, get it done, no excuses.

Did you know you can push people harder, and get better results than they even knew possible? It's true – until they break. Until that plan backfires, and blows up in your face, and your entire company is burning to the ground.

But the manager can't possibly figure out what's wrong, with the littered fragments of broken employees strewn about. "These people are useless," the manager thinks and replaces the whole lot. Rinse, cycle, repeat. A whole other crop of successes are then ripped and torn to shreds.

—

There is the simple, glaring answer. It's to let people work on what they love.

The statistics support this too. When people are fully invested and love their work, profits rise – 20% over the competitors run like a military unit.

That's a stunning number, 20%. For this consumeristic world we live in, one driven by profits, and insane revenue growth projections, why are so many companies leaving this solution off the table? It makes absolutely no sense.

100% of companies should be run this way – to hire people who have a passion for their work. To let their "employees" run wild and chase their passions with unlimited ambition – because it works, and because it ultimately impacts the bottom line.

—

Here's the thing too – I've seen this first hand, with real dollars. It's one thing to look at a study, but it's another to live the experience.

I've seen salespeople continually outperform their peers, simply because they "love what they do" and are given the freedom to use their strengths.

The sales world is such that you can teach a monkey to do it – almost quite literally. "Call these people, dial for numbers, send and respond to emails, capture orders." It's all robotic and ratio driven. But when you have a salesperson running free, thinking outside the box, and allowed to do the job how they want – revenues instantly increase – 20%. It's like magic.

—

If you're a company or a manager, you're no dummy – you also understand the concept of compounding interest. If you have a company, or salesperson, increase revenue 20%, year over year, that equates to such larger growth, as the 20% builds on itself every cycle.

Compounding interest is a rocket ship to the moon.

If you want to have exciting sales, and unbelievable growth, give your employees the freedom to do what they want.

I promise you – it'll be the best business decision you ever made. And your employees will be grateful too.

CHOOSE A PASSION

I'm a writer.

That feels good to say, yet also weird.

I'm not a professional writer like a journalist or New York Times best-selling author (at least not yet anyway).

So, what qualifies me as a writer, is that I write.

I put words on a page, both in physical form and digitally, and share my thoughts with others.

That's all it takes to be a writer. To write.

—

If you wanted to take up any hobby, like a painter for instance, I think it's fair to say you qualify as a painter if you put colors on an easel.

Even if you're only going in your garage and tossing buckets of paint against a board, I say if you want to call yourself a painter, you have every right.

So go ahead. Paint.

—

Even though I claim to be a writer, and love making a career out of it, it hasn't always been that way.

I didn't come out of the womb writing. I wasn't a child-prodigy crafting sonnets. And I'm definitely not a Stephen King type writer with stratospheric book advances and fame rocketing to the moon.

I kind of suck. And I'm a hack.

But I really love what I do.

—

I tried to remember when I decided to write full-time and make it a part of my life.

Because honestly, I had always been writing, in one form or another.

There were assignments in elementary school to write stories. We'd publish them and pass them to our friends.

In college, I'd jot my thoughts down in a journal and have fun doing it. This was before blogs ever existed.

So there were plenty of instances of being able to write and enjoying it – but it wasn't such a linear and obvious path.

—

After college, I was trying to find myself and exploring different careers. Many of those careers didn't pan out, and that's ok, but I kept trying.

Once I had a burning desire to be a stand-up comedian. I took a class and did some shows. I really enjoyed that a lot.

Getting on stage and receiving laughs from people wasn't as fulfilling as I originally thought. It was just fine. I could take or leave it – I wasn't passionate about it.

What I did love though, was the joke writing process.

I remember those days clearly, much more than the stand-up performances.

It'd be a Saturday morning, and I'd sit on my porch and outline jokes for 2 hours. It was such an enjoyable and addicting process.

I enjoyed it so much, I even considered joke writing as a career path – which I totally could have succeeded in.

But my takeaway was that I truly loved to write.

—

So while I was in another miserable job, I decided to write a novel. I figured how hard could it be.

The answer, obviously, is incredibly hard.

But I had read lots of published garbage that wasn't very good. Lots of professional writing felt sophomoric at best.

And I figured, if they could publish those monkeys, then they'd definitely publish my first crack at novel writing. Because I tell good stories. Duh.

But man, was I wrong.

That first novel was unreadable. It was so awful. I couldn't even bother to share it with anyone because it made no sense.

I remember it clearly too because it was a cross between *Hunger Games* and *Dragon Ball Z*. It was about a bunch of ninja kids who get abducted by aliens to fight in an arena to save the world. It was epic.

But it sucked.

—

But then I was hooked.

The writing process had been so soothing and exhilarating. It was so much fun to create a story in my head.

I just desperately needed to figure how to get better at writing and how to make a career out of it.

Because for me, nothing else in life feels quite the same as writing does.

And every time I try to leave it all behind, it keeps pulling me back, like an awful drug addiction, convincing me I'm not done, and that I have more stories in me, and more to say.

—

So the moral of the story, and the answer for how to find your passion, is to follow your gut and try new things.

I had an absolute burning passion to try stand-up comedy. I didn't know why. I just seemed like a cool gig at the time and I could perhaps make a career out of it.

Obviously, it didn't pan out, but that's not the point.

It led me to my real career and my real passion of writing.

If I had never tried comedy, or the 10 other risky endeavors before it, I would never have found my gifts.

—

I had always been someone who "wants a passion." I'd even be angry at people who found there's.

Like what makes them so special or gifted to work on what they love, and to make lots of money doing it?

So, yeah, I was jealous.

But I also think there's too much pressure on millennials and college graduates to immediately find their talents. Like you have to pick the correct college, and the correct major, or else your life will suck.

None of that is true. It's just a marketing ploy by colleges to take your money.

But do take the education you have, and the ability to learn new things, and go try new stuff.

I think the newly crafted Fiction Writing degrees and MFA courses are a load of crap. These degrees will leave you more frustrated than anything, as there are no jobs in fiction writing. It's not like there are giant corporations hiring writers out of college to write books for them. That's not a thing, and probably shouldn't be.

I didn't even decide to pursue writing until I was 30 years old.

That's like 7 years of trying to write every day, writing crappy novels, and short stories. It's a lot of work. It's not an overnight success. It's not something a degree can do for you.

—

So, if you feel you're called to do something – maybe even God is calling you – go and do it.

And sometimes things don't work out. Sometimes they fail. But don't try something new, wanting it to fail. You need to succeed, you need to get better, and stronger, and find new ways of thinking.

But inevitably failure does come – know that it'll be ok, and no one will judge you.

Because, at least for me, finding a passion was a wobbly journey, from one strange pursuit to the next.

But if I never pursued being a comedian, and still walked around today with a desire to pursue that, I think I'd be very upset with myself and an angry person, for never trying – so don't be that way.

Rip your passions like a bandaid, be brave, and see where they lead you.

Perhaps you'll be amazed.

And perhaps you'll find your passion.

PEOPLE ARE HORRIBLE

People drive me nuts.

One minute I'll be minding my own business, having a grand old time, then the next someone is crashing into me – into my precious space – and driving me bat-sh*t crazy.

I'm pretty sure, we'd all be better off alone.

—

Last Friday, I was relieved to leave work. Fridays are always the best day of work (because weekend, duh), and should be considered a holy day.

On top of that, I had just completed a difficult project and felt good about my accomplishment.

But wouldn't you know it, in the middle of my good mood, some idiot cut me off at a traffic light.

It's not like I died, but the terror of having to slam on your brakes because someone isn't paying attention always gets your blood boiling.

—

"It'll be ok," I said to myself, as I continued on my way home.

Not only 100 yards away, I got into a second altercation.

There's an intersection near my house, with 10 lanes of traffic, all trying to navigate a 4-way stop. Half the time, someone's honking at someone else because they're doing it wrong.

Well, guess what, I traveled through on my merry way – with the right of way mind you – and some (not) lovely lady decided to lay on her horn for a good 30 seconds.

What is it exactly you're honking at? Because I have the right of way? You want me to reverse and try this all over again?

Geez lady. Chill out.

—

So all that nonsense ruined a perfectly good Friday evening. I even woke up Saturday morning wanting to kill those people.

How dare they ruin my good mood, and my weekend, of all things. The nerve.

—

So then Sunday came around and I was feeling much better.

I wanted to go to church to gobble up the good word of God and be on my holy way.

Do I even need to extrapolate what happened next? (But thankfully no, it wasn't another car incident)

The worst behaved church attendees are the ones who arrive 30 minutes late, sit right behind you, then carry on an hour-long conversation for the duration of the church service.

What nerve, these people.

I had the thought to move, and in retrospect probably should have. But for the sake of being "kind," I didn't want to create a scene.

Regardless, I turned around at one point, to see if this was really happening to me. I figured the people would have been brand new also, so that was the other half of my reasoning to be kind.

I could only imagine a visitor coming to church for the first time, only to get chewed out by a psychotic man who demands silence. I'm sure they'd write a lengthy blog post about it too.

But no, that wasn't the case. They were wearing volunteer team t-shirts. Clearly members of the congregation. Clearly aware of "church etiquette."

But what the hell was wrong with these people and why were they bothering me?

—

That evening, I was looking forward to a nice dinner with my wife.

She chose a fancy "adult" dinner place (which will not be named). We treated it like a date.

The atmosphere in the restaurant was excellent – dark mood lighting, some candlelight, and an appropriate roar of jovial conversation from other diners.

That was until an infant got plopped right on my left shoulder.

What the hell? "Who brings a kid to a place like this?" I said aloud.

The kid quickly turned the table into her personal drum-set and cheered loudly to provide backup vocals. She was like a regular rock band.

Ok, fine. Whatever. She'll chill out in a minute.

Except a minute later a lady came crashing through, bumping into our chairs, to navigate a massive stroller into the middle of the restaurant.

A second table, with three(!) toddlers, got sat right on the other side of us.

We were now surrounded by children.

The new table that arrived turned the place into a screaming match.

I couldn't take it anymore. We had to get out of there.

—

What is with all these people?

Are they mentally handicapped? Do they not understand social norms?

I literally don't get it.

The only explanation I care to figure is that everyone is in a bad mood.

I know how I feel most of the time when I'm in a job I hate, or a circumstance I can't change. I trudge around the world with a cloud of gloom following me.

I tell myself that everyone else feels exactly the same way.

Maybe on a Friday night, people are exhausted and rushing home after a hard day of work.

Maybe they're not paying attention, can't focus anymore, and absentmindedly zoom through a traffic light.

Or maybe they're so frustrated, they take their anger out on the next person who crosses their path, and lays on their horn for 30 seconds because they're losing their mind.

Or maybe everyone at church is already broken, and that's why they need a church. Maybe they've just had the worst week of their life, and the message and community at church is the one ray of hope they get.

Or maybe moms and dads are exhausted and sleep deprived from raising screaming toddlers – at their wit's end – and all they want to do after a long exhausting week is go to a fancy dinner. They can't even hear the kids anymore. After all, they've become deaf-tone to the noise.

—

A part of me wishes everyone would behave in public. I, personally, want to be left alone.

Sadly, as a society, we're never going to get there.

Because everyone is hurt. Everyone is broken. Everyone is exhausted and tired. Or everyone is trying to behave like they have it all together. Or aren't stressed about money, bills, or personal problems.

We all have these masks on, pretending like we're ok. When on the inside we're torn apart.

—

So yeah, the next time someone is rude to you, or cuts you off in traffic, or is too loud for your liking – just know that everyone is struggling.

You don't need to hold a grudge, or get revenge.

Chances are, those people are already worse off than you.

And more than anything, they probably need your compassion or your help.

But they're too angry – or prideful – to ask.

DESIRE TO WIN

I walked a 5k and got a medal for my effort.

I shook my head at the ridiculousness of it all – it was literally a participation trophy.

At the finish line, the race volunteer presented the medal over my head.

"I don't want that," I barked, "I came in dead last." Because I had a chest full of air and wasn't tired in the least.

"But you participated and you made it," he encouraged me. He followed through with his job regardless and chucked the medal around my neck.

He literally lamented, the "I participated," so here's my reward.

A literal participation trophy.

WTF has this world come to?

—

I didn't mind the 5k at all.

It was a TurkeyTrot on Thanksgiving morning, and we intentionally signed up to be walkers. The entrance fee was less, as there wasn't a timed chip in our race-bibs.

But we also wanted to bring our dog, BooBoo, because he's a knucklehead and needed the exercise.

The event was great though. I have absolutely no complaints.

It was a pleasant morning and cool for Florida standards.

Besides, it's become a tradition to go out there and get some fresh air before the carnivorous festivities begin.

It's fun.

—

But what gets me are those trophies.

It took me over an hour to walk 3 miles. Why am I getting rewarded for that?

If I go on an hour walk outside my house, no one is there to greet me with a medal on my return.

We should all be walkers. We should all be active.

It's amazing how much better you feel when you regularly exercise – regardless of weight loss issues.

—

Medals should be reserved for winners.

During the 5k, after 15 minutes I checked my phone and saw we were a quarter through the course.

"I wonder when the first place runner will finish?" I said aloud.

Seconds later, we heard loud cheering back at the starting line – which also doubled as the finish.

Two men were in a deadlock sprint, gunning down the final stretch and racing each other to the end.

I was stunned. It's one of those images that'll be burned in my memory for all time.

To see these guys, on Thanksgiving morning, give it their all and run at an absolute sprint – just for the chance to win.

And it's not like we're talking about the Olympics here – the world's fastest runners probably burn through 3 miles in 10 minutes.

The guys racing for the finish, were only going for local fame, and personal pride.

I'm sure they'd be the talk around the office water cooler on Monday, having just won the Turkey Trot.

—

That certainly deserves a medal.

You trained hard for a race and beat a crowd of people. Congratulations. You win.

That's how medals should work.

Instead, I took my sweet time with my wife, chatting about life, took pictures with our dog, and took too long water breaks at every station – for the dog, obviously.

Yet, as we crossed an arbitrary finish line, we were also presented with a reward.

The same reward the winners got.

Why?

—

There's some damage this "participation trophy" era is having on society.

Maybe it's all the standardized tests we put our kids through – to learn the absolute basic skills without striving to learn more.

Maybe it's bosses that give you fake praise for accomplishing work – even though it's literally our job. "Congratulations. You did the job we're paying you to do." What?

It's having an underlying effect on our lives, as we show up to work, or anything really, and do the bare minimum to get by.

That's not really a satisfying way to live.

—

My wife is an idea generator.

All sorts of ideas fly off the top of her head – maybe creative concepts, or mostly business ideas.

We joke about our future kids and how we'll feel sorry for them.

With all the business jargon sputtered in our house, through osmosis, without having to try, they'll learn how to run a startup company by age 5.

We won't be spending weekends on the soccer pitch or softball field. We'll be at hackathons or robotics competitions.

I'm sort of joking. I don't really know – and my point isn't that we'll push them in any direction. I do want my kids to be well-rounded and learn lots of different skills.

I want to raise kids that are self-reliant, and able to fend for themselves. They'll be able to start a business or do whatever they want.

The point is for them to escape the grubby turmoil of Corporate America, and do whatever they please instead.

—

One of my favorite organizations is the Girl Scouts.

The cookies are delicious, obviously, but what the girls gain from entrepreneurship is invaluable.

It seems like lots of parents are forced to participate too, which I don't really understand. Granted, business and sales are hard, so it is a little far-fetched to believe a 10-year-old will understand the precepts of world domination.

But my favorite girl scout came while we were sitting outside a brewery.

She came up pulling her wagon stacked high with cookie boxes, and she didn't even need to ask for sales.

I quickly shouted at her and bought two right away – Samoa and Thin Mint – because those are the best.

But that's stuff I like to see kids do. Load up a wagon and sell them at a brewery.

Don't even ask permission. Screw the brewer. If he kicks you out, ask for forgiveness. But don't be so timid to think you aren't welcome, little girl with delicious cookies, because you are.

And all those tipsy patrons are starving and hankering for a box of cookies. So good on you for identifying your target market.

Because that's a skill that'll serve you better in life, and you'll be able to write your own path to success.

BETTER WAY TO LIVE

This is about exercise.

Listen – exercise is extremely important. And I'm not just talking about weight loss.

I actually have no idea about losing weight – I'm a super skinny dude – so that's not my expertise.

If you're concerned about shedding pounds, there are a million self-help and diet books on the shelves. I'm not sure the world needs another fad diet anyway.

So what I'm talking about now, is specifically to people who "think they are healthy."

The skinny people. People who look like me.

—

One of the blessings (and curses) of being skinny, is I tell myself I can eat whatever I want.

I don't have food cravings, so it takes a great deal of abuse to gain any sort of weight.

The one time I succeed in gaining a few pounds, I found myself eating lunch at McDonald's every day, then greasy diner food at night. Basically a steady diet of delicious french fries.

I literally stopped eating that way and lost the weight immediately.

—

That's not to make anyone feel bad who does struggle with

those issues.

It's only to paint the picture that I don't pay attention to what I eat.

Like last year I was eating a bag of M&Ms every afternoon. I'd switch it up between the peanut M&Ms and the ones with the peanut butter center – I loved those.

Then I'd go home each night and have a beer. Science says 1-2 alcoholic drinks a day is ok for you, so it felt healthy enough.

And then I'd eat a cookie.

Anyone who knows anything about dieting would say I was a moron. That what I was eating was unhealthy.

But being so skinny, it doesn't affect me the same way. So I hardly cared.

That's my self-talk too – "I'm skinny. I can eat whatever I want."

—

After a Memorial Day weekend of drinking too many beers, I didn't feel so well.

It took a few days to feel better again, as the body has a hard time recovering when you get older. It's not like I'm in my 20s anymore.

So I thought, "I don't feel good. Why am I drinking beer every day anyway?"

On top of not feeling good, my day job was miserable – like always.

I would go to work depressed, then go home at night and have a beer. And repeat the process all week.

I didn't feel fulfilled. Or that I was living the life God called for me.

—

After a little research, I found alcohol and depression go hand-in-hand.

It's common for alcoholics to fall into depression. But it's also common for depressed people to turn to alcohol.

It's a vicious cycle that sucks people from both sides and keeps you stuck in its grasp.

It's a hard trap to escape too.

—

But so I took a hard look at what I was doing and decided I really didn't need to drink a beer every night.

I'd experiment, and give it up, and see what that looked like.

As with any routine – or addiction – the first few days were tough. But after that, I started to feel much better.

If that simple change could help, what else could I do to feel better?

The answer was exercise.

—

It's common knowledge about the "runner's high." It's the feeling you get after a run, that you can take over the world.

A runner's high is great, but it's not the only reason to be healthy.

Exercising makes me feel better at work. My brain is sharper and I'm less sluggish.

I'm able to push through hard tasks all day, where I barely had an hours worth of energy before.

It means I can tackle projects on the weekend and have enough energy leftover.

It means I'm a better person.

And all I'm doing is going for a run.

—

Honestly though, here's what I'm focusing on:

Exercise regularly – a run every other day, with a long walk in between – because walks are fun and refreshing.

No coffee. I'm always on-again, off-again with the caffeine. But it really messes with my brain, and the effects wane after 14 days anyway, so caffeine is a liar.

No beer. Ok, not totally "no beer," but no beer during the week. On the weekend I can have one at a social setting. But there's no point in sitting around my house drinking beer by myself. It just doesn't make me feel good.

No sugar. Again, like the beer – all things in moderation. I'd eat the M&Ms every day because I was tired and needed energy. But that was a lie. The extra sugar makes me feel awful. But having a cookie every now and again (like once a month) is perfectly fine.

—

Now I feel like a chameleon because there are two different people living inside me.

There's the one who's lethargic, who barely has the energy to wake up every morning. He hates his job, sits in a cubicle all day, eats too much candy, and drinks beer every night.

Then there's the one who has tons of energy, feels great all day long, and has ideas flowing through his head like a fire hydrant. He's excited about life and the work he gets to do. He's also more friendly. All it takes too is a small dedication to running for 30 minutes. And not drinking beer all the time.

But that, my friends, feels like a world of difference for such a small sacrifice.

—

And I'm still skinny. I look like the exact same person in both cases.

But it's what's on the inside that counts – that you can't see.

So even if someone looks skinny, and you can't figure why they're exercising – it probably has nothing to do with weight loss.

Even though they appear to have it all together on the outside, it doesn't mean they aren't hurting on the inside.

—

A study followed children who exercise and those who don't.

Not surprisingly, kids who regularly get 70 minutes of exercise – whether recess, organized sports, or unstructured playtime – received better grades. They became smarter.

The researcher went on to suggest a school day should be structured with a 45 minute lesson, followed by 15 minutes of recess.

Wow. Could you imagine if school was actually like that? I think so many more kids would enjoy the day, instead of being locked in a "prison" all day, suffering under fluorescent lights, learning about long division.

But it makes sense to teach kids the way we do – locking them inside for 6 hours – we're training them to sit in cubicles for the rest of their life. (There's a heavy dose of sarcasm in that sentence, I hope you're picking up...)

—

Exercise is important for your brain.

It's important for your soul.

So I hope you can take some gentle advice, and get some refreshing air for your overall well-being, not just your waistline.

Maybe your career – or passion – will thank you.

WORLD OF HURT

I complain about everything.

I didn't think I do – I feel optimistic about pursuits, and goals, and dreams – but when it comes down to it, I'm a master complainer.

National bestselling author and award-winning podcaster Tim Ferris recognized this behavior and launched a 21 Day No Complaint Challenge.

In it, he goes 21 days without complaining and documents the outcome.

At first, I thought it was ridiculous. Like, how much better could life be without complaining, and it is even possible? Like, if something bad happens, how are you to not complain? Is that even natural?

Complaining feels as commonplace as breathing – it just exists.

So I began guarding my thoughts and contemplating what I was thinking about and why.

I soon realized I do complain a lot – and for no good reason.

Like this morning, I decided I didn't like my shoes. Why? I don't know. They're perfectly fine shoes, but they annoy my feet and make me feel off-balance. And they're old. They're not new anymore. I need new shoes.

Then I hated my car. My car sucks. It's old. The stereo doesn't sound crisp and the sun visor is broken. I need a new car.

Then I hated the person who cut me off in traffic, then the second person to cut me off, and the guy who left his blinker on for far too long. I hated them all and they ruined my morning commute.

And don't get me started on my job – let's just say I'm not pleased. But hardly a day goes by when this isn't the case. I'm rarely, if ever, grateful for my job. I hate my job – always. It's like a calling card. It's my claim to fame.

Alright, so I was wrong on the complaining front. I do complain a lot. There's actually not a lot I'm particularly grateful for if I'm honest.

—

I do a morning routine of journaling. It's not a diary – it's not a reconciliation of the day's events – it's a brain dump. It gets the junk out of my head.

In it, I'm allowed to write whatever I want – it doesn't matter. I can write anything. I can write, "I don't have anything to write," 50 times and that would suffice. As long as I get three pages complete, I've succeeded.

But a strange thing happens when I alter my thoughts. When I'm in a foul mood, and all I have are negative emotions running through my blood, it feels cathartic to release those emotions and get them squared away. Obviously, these are negative thoughts, but it helps to release them and not have them bottled up and bouncing around in my head all day.

Sometimes though, starting my morning with negative feelings follow me the rest of the day.

When that happens, I try and catch myself, and right the ship.

Because the inverse is also true.

When I ignore the pain I'm in – and focus on what I'm truly grateful for – I feel like a new man.

Sometimes the journaling is a list of grateful things, and I feel like a holy warrior. I feel like I can take on the world and no one can defeat me.

The other day I was grateful for the path I am on, and the realization of repeated mistakes, and of pursuing the wrong thing, and of ultimately pride issues. And it made me cry.

Just flipping that one switch in the morning, from complaining to gratitude, felt like a weight had been lifted off my chest and all the world's problems had melted away. And I hadn't done one tangible thing, I hadn't lifted a finger or changed my circumstance.

All I had done was write – and write about positive things.

—

Listen, I'm not going to pretend to be an expert in this subject matter, but only in how I feel and what happens to me.

It's comparable to the media I consume, and how it makes me feel afterward.

If I dive into a scary movie or a horror novel – at the moment it feels fun to be alive, like you've survived a roller coaster and came out stronger. But after, those thoughts linger. Somehow I begin to focus on "dark" things. Things like death, and murder, and killing, and guns. Is any of that really beneficial to anyone? Does it make anyone a better person?

But when I consume wholesome media – uplifting stories about people doing compelling things – like RJ Palacio's *Wonder*, or Jen Hatmaker's *Interrupted*, Ann Voskamp's blog – these things with a positive message – it makes me feel better. I feel like a better person, with a life worth living and fighting for.

Literally, when we focus on the horror of our lives – the pain, the suffering, the negativity – it consumes us and pours out of our veins. It rules our lives. It defines us.

But if we choose compassion and gratitude, our life drastically shifts in the opposite direction – we become filled with peace and hope and forgiveness.

When we are "poked" in life, we no longer have the gut reaction of spilling the venom inside. Instead, we stop, reflect, and begin to help whoever had "bumped" into our lives.

Because there are plenty of hurting people out there – crashing into each other – and just waiting for an answer or a savior to come.

OVERCOMING PROCRASTINATION

Overcoming procrastination takes effort. We're all master procrastinators and have spent years avoiding work. We put things off until tomorrow, feeling like we'll have more energy in the future.

We make bargains with ourselves, thinking today is not the right day.

Maybe it's our job, errands, or tasks at home. Whatever it is, tomorrow always feels like the better response. We convince ourselves, "Tomorrow I won't be tired, tomorrow I'll have more time, tomorrow I'll have more money."

But you know what? Tomorrow always comes, and it looks exactly like today.

And then we repeat the cycle, putting off work, and making ourselves miserable. All day. Every day.

—

As a college student, I hated Sunday night. Sunday night was the worst. It seemed like the most fun was had on Sunday night.

The best TV shows were on, great football games, and my friends were doing fun things.

But the problem with Sunday night is Monday morning is hours away.

I felt like I had a plague of material due on Monday, and no one else did. No matter the course I took – whether it be Computer Science or Math – there was always a project due on Monday.

It was like my teachers all ganged up and decided to load their syllabuses with Monday heavy due dates. It felt like they were out to get me.

—

"Hey Joe, we're going to play floor hockey in the gym. Want to play?" No, I can't. I have to sit in the computer lab and fix this bug.

"Hey Joe, we're all jamming ourselves in a tiny car and going out for frozen custard. Want to come?" I can't. I have to write an essay on the synoptic gospels.

There was always something fun happening and I felt like the biggest loser. Who wants to do work on a Sunday night, when all their friends are out playing?

I certainly didn't. And I blamed all my professors.

It was everyone else's fault, except my own.

—

Sunday night was torture for three years. It was the worst feeling in the world.

Until finally, senior year, I figured out how to overcome that dread.

I made a bargain with myself to never do homework on the weekend. I decided to only work Monday through Friday. If the work wasn't done by Friday night, then it wasn't getting done.

And there would be no rushing on Monday morning. The work was either going to be done, or it wasn't. It was a pass or fail endeavor.

Let me tell you, that discipline isn't easy. Often times, late on a

Friday afternoon, I'd find myself in the library, writing a report. My friends would be lounging around, playing Xbox. But I'd be banging out my homework like a robot.

Do you know what ended up happening? My weekends became 1,000 times more fun. There was no longer this dread about the work needing to be done on Sunday. No more thinking about the project I had been putting off. I had already accomplished my goal on Friday – when no one else was working – and freed up my entire weekend.

—

Then the flip side of the coin began to rear its ugly head. Late on Sunday night, while my friends would be grinding to finish last minute projects, I'd be lying around, watching a movie, or doing lots of nothing. It pissed them off to no end.

"Don't you ever have work to do?" They'd ask.

"I already did it," I'd reply.

They never believed me. They thought I had an easy workload and were jealous. Little did they know I had been working harder than them all week long.

—

As a college student, that's a discipline that took me four years to develop. No one told me to do it. It became apparent from my Sunday night dread, that there was a better way to get work done.

If you're looking for a magic bullet to procrastination, it's "don't wait."

You know what things are piling up and are bothering you. The only way to relieve the pain is to rip the band-aid and get it done today.

Make a plan. Make a contract with yourself. And allow yourself to enjoy the relief and excitement on the other side.

And remember, we all have horrible work that needs to get done. It's not pleasant. But one way or another it has to be addressed.

It's up to you. You have to decide.

Do you want to do the work on a Friday or a Sunday night?

LEARN NEW THINGS

Is there a trick to learn new things? It seems like people are either talented or they're not.

Because we all envy other people. We look at their skills and accomplishments and it makes us jealous.

We're jealous because we feel cheated at life like we lost the life-lottery and weren't born in the right country or to the right parents. We're mad that we weren't pushed as kids and forced to be a doctor.

But you know what? There's nothing that another person has done, that you can't figure out how to do for yourself.

—

My hardest class in high school was Senior Physics. Senior Physics kicked my butt.

For one, physics is sort of an absolute science. There's a bunch of rules and a lot of math.

Gravity? You mean you can crunch some numbers to figure out gravitational forces? It hurts your brain just thinking about it.

The actual course subject was one thing, but the way it was presented was another.

My teacher forced us to learn on our own. At the time it felt like absolute torture, but it was one of the best gifts I've ever received in life.

—

Let's get one thing straight: High school is easy. I think I took a nap during most of my classes and passed just by having a heartbeat.

High school teachers stand up front and verbally tell you everything. They're like, "Hey this is how you conjugate this Spanish verb, now let's do it together. I'll show you how."

You'd have to be a moron to not appreciate this hand holding.

But high school is an anomaly. This is not how life works.

For those of you wanting to drop out of high school, you need a reality check. High school is a cakewalk. The rest of life is so much harder.

—

But that physics class, he made us read out of the textbook and teach ourselves! Oh, the humanity! That should be a crime in 48 states!

That felt really hard. It was a hard class. I had a hard time passing and I was pissed off all the time.

I was glad to finally graduate, and be done with that torture. It was finally time to move on to college where I could chase my wildest dreams and cure world hunger.

—

Guess what? If high school is a cakewalk, college is like getting that cake forced down your throat with a firehose. You're like drowning and choking on the delicious sugary dessert and desperately want the pain to stop.

Fall semester, freshman year of college, I had a hard time.

Sure, some classes were simple and reminiscent of high school.

But lots of them weren't.

Calculus was like a deer in the headlights. The professor would briefly show a problem, then make us learn it on our own.

Oh, and there was no assigned homework. At first, I thought that aspect was great. There were "suggested" problems to solve, but we didn't have to hand anything in.

As difficult as the Calculus subject matter was, I at least enjoyed the easy workload. No homework felt like a dream.

That was, until, the first test came. My grade: "F." I failed, straight up. I think I got a zero.

I wasn't use to failing, so that hurt. But I also didn't know how to fix it. I figured I'd try again or listen harder to the teacher.

Then the next test: "F."

This was becoming a royal nightmare.

—

Because I'm stubborn, I stuck with the course. A wise student would have dropped it, so a bad grade wouldn't affect their record, but that's not how I roll.

I like to stare failure in the face. I like to think I can overcome anything.

The professor kindly pulled me aside and said, "Listen, you need an A on the final to pass the course."

So that was my challenge. In the span of Finals Week, I was determined to learn all the Calculus problems I had been avoiding an entire semester.

And you know what? I did it. It sucked a lot and I had to study late into the night. Every night. I had to ask upperclassmen in my dorm for help. I had to fight, scratch, and kick my way into the Final Exam.

The Final Exam came and I was ready. I had the world's most

detailed cheat-sheet with the tiniest of writing, but I was ready. I had learned Calculus and I was ready.

I got a "C+" on the Final. Far away from my goal. But I was incredibly proud of my effort.

And now I had actually learned the material. I knew how Calculus worked. I felt like the professor would pass me just because of my apparent overnight success.

Nope. As a final grade for the course, I got a "D+."

Ugh. At least I hadn't totally failed, but I would need to take the class again in the spring.

But this time, I'd be ready.

—

Learning things isn't easy, but it can be done.

The biggest lesson I learned from college was how to teach myself anything. I don't remember anything about Calculus or any of the ridiculous classes they make you take.

But that's not the point. It's that you've suffered through four years of trials, forcing yourself to learn new concepts, and to pass arbitrary tests proving your mastery of the subject.

Is the college experience worth the cost? Yes, definitely. But is it prerequisite to learn things in life? Absolutely not.

You have the power to learn new things. You are your own obstacle. Read a book, practice, and find other people who are successful.

If there's a dream you want to chase, go after it, and teach yourself the necessary skills.

There's no dream out there that's too impossible to pursue. Because there's already another person who's done it, paving the way for you.

TAKING RISKS

Trying new things is hard. We're always stuck in our routines. We know what we like and what we don't.

But how would your world change if you tried something new? Even if you didn't want to?

—

When I was interning for Disney, I had a day off. It felt like we worked all the time, and at strange hours, so any time off was a blessing.

Half the time we'd play in the park on our downtime. That may sound like fun, but it gets old after the 20th time you've ridden It's A Small World, and you're no longer enamored with the size of the Earth – it's actually a pretty big planet, after all.

One day I wanted to do something different. Being a Saturday, I decided to go get donuts. Because Saturday is like "donut day," obviously.

I wrangled up my friends and was like, "Hey, who wants to get donuts?" They said yes. They thought it was the most brilliant idea ever.

We piled into my minivan as I began to recall my love of the Boston cream donut from Dunkin Donuts. That was my goal – to get the Boston cream. It is the best donut in the world.

Then someone peeped up and argued against me.

"Have you ever tried Krispy Kreme? It's better." They said.

What is a crispy cream? I had not heard of it. It sounded like a crispy ice cream stand full of ice chunks. I wasn't interested.

Regardless, I played along. We were on an adventure, after all, exploring the surrounding of Lake Buena Vista.

—

We first stopped at Dunkin Donuts and picked up a dozen. There were plenty to share as we had other roommates to feed.

I got my Boston cream and was happy. It was everything I hoped for and dreamed.

Then, begrudgingly, I continued to this fabled crispy donut spot. It sounded like a gross local place.

No one even knew where it was either. This was before GPS and we had to look up the address and a map. This was like the dark ages before the internet – very confusing times.

So, after driving around aimlessly, we found it. It was on the outskirts of town where the "non-Disney" people live.

I was still skeptical, and scared, as the Krispy Kreme looked like a 1950s doo-opp diner – just like every other tacky Orlando attraction.

I was ready to order a dozen assorted donuts, wanting to flee as fast as possible, when the swift employees intervened.

"If you've never been here," they said, "You need to try the original glazed."

I hate glazed donuts. I've been born and raised on Dunkin Donuts products like every good New England boy – and everyone knows glazed donuts suck. Only old people and the homeless eat glazed donuts.

Still, trying to "go with the flow" and not irritate my band of fellow donut seekers, I backed down. I agreed to eat the glazed.

—

"Be careful, it's hot off the fryer," the employee said.

Why would I eat a hot donut? That sounds disgusting. Everyone knows good donuts are cold.

But then I ate it, and my world changed. Suddenly my mouth was filled with the sweet sugary goodness of a piping hot Krispy Kreme donut.

"That's amazing!" I screamed and ate another.

Then we had to figure out how many to order. "People normally eat 4 or more," they said. How is that possible? No one can eat 4 donuts. But as I soon discovered, with these thin flavorful puffs of flaky clouds, you can jam a bunch in your pie hole and still be hungry.

So we left and my worldview of donuts had entirely changed. I was pleasantly surprised with our out-of-the-way adventure and discovery of amazing food.

Also, now that it was nearing lunchtime, we had to eat lunch. So we stopped at Pizza Hut and bought a stuffed crust pizza – because that makes sense after multiple donuts.

We arrived back to the apartments with our arms filled with donuts and pizza. Our roommates looked at us like we were insane, and when we began to shout our praises of the Krispy Kreme goodness, they looked at us with disgust.

So with disgusting sugary carbs swirling about our tummies, we settled in the living room and watched Star Wars.

Because that's what trying something new is all about. Filling your day with donuts, pizza, Star Wars, and friends.

And having someone to jolt us from our comfort zone – what else do you really need in life?

PERFECT DAY

Does a perfect day exist? What would that day look like? Is it practical or a fantasy?

What would it mean to live an ideal day? What if you could wake up tomorrow and have the best day of your life?

—

I've experienced my perfect day, and I love it.

Bizarrely, it's only occurred when I'm unemployed. When I'm between jobs, looking for more work, I'm having the time of my life.

Granted, I'm generally broke during these days – so that's an issue – but my actual waking and working hours are filled with happiness and peace.

I get up at an appropriate time. I don't sleep for too long and don't wake too early. Falling asleep at 11 PM and waking at 7 AM feels appropriate. Not too much, and not too little – just the right amount.

As soon as I wake I hit the shower. I can't function until I've had a shower. I'm sure there are scientific reasons, but when I miss my shower, I feel like a hobo. I feel dirty, and my head also never truly wakes up. I feel like a zombie all day.

I stand in the shower and think. There's no real structure to this, other than I let my mind race and figure things out. But it lessens the pain of being tired, and I come out refreshed.

Joe Shaughnessy

—

Then I do my morning routine. I eat breakfast, listen to music, read the Bible, journal, pray, and exercise. That may sound like a lot, but it only takes an hour. And it makes a world of difference.

The days that I journal are filled with optimism and hope. The days I skip it or sleep in, are filled with dread. Utter terror and despair.

So it's important I get it done.

—

After that, it's time to work.

I turn on the computer and prepare to write.

I do this funny thing where my computer isn't connected to the internet. Any crazy distractions, like Windows updates or notifications, drive me insane. It even helps to tempt me from surfing the internet looking at random sites.

I can do all that later. I can check Facebook and ESPN later. For right now, it's time to write.

So I bang out an hour's worth of fiction. And that's it. Whatever my writing goal is for the day, I hit it, then stop. No more, no less.

I make an agreement with myself, that I can screw around after I hit the goal.

But it seems like every day I sit down to work, it feels like I'll never succeed.

Staring at that blank screen is terrifying. I think whatever I have accomplished in the past, I will never be able to reproduce again. Doubt creeps into my mind.

The easier option is to quit, or surf the internet, or read a book.

It feels like every day I sit down to write, is the most difficult day of my life. Like I'm a phony and a fake.

But then it happens. The words inevitably flow and I'm in the zone.

I really enjoy the writing session and an hour later feel like I've won the lottery. I feel like I just wrote the most amazing piece of fiction in the history of the world and people will pay me millions of dollars for my stories.

Ultimately, most of the stuff I write is crap. But that's ok. It allows me to pick the diamonds in the rough and run with what's great – and to toss what's not.

—

Then I take a break. I eat a banana.

It's important to take breaks in your day. If you work for 8 straight hours you'll go insane. So don't do that. Take lots of mini-breaks throughout the day and you'll feel amazing.

So then I get back to work. If I'm looking for a job, I'm blasting out my portfolio and resume. Or I might edit, or blog, or have other real work to do.

If the morning writing session is the most important thing I have to do that day, then the following hour is the second most important. I don't wait. Whatever it is, just get it done.

Because ultimately, I want to have a leisurely afternoon.

If I work hard in the morning, I feel at ease in the afternoon. Because sometimes after lunch I'm tired and want to take a nap. And it's ok to rest. I've already accomplished the most important thing and can do whatever I want.

Sometimes though, there are other work issues that pop up, or emails to send, or phone calls to return. This is a great time for these time-suck energy-wasting activities. They do need to get done, eventually, but not before other more important items.

—

But then sometimes my day frees up. There's nothing else to do and it's a great day outside, so I go for a bike ride. Or a run. I just get to do something physical, that I enjoy, that wakes up my mind and makes me feel great.

For me, a run in the afternoon is fun. Any other time is torture.

Once everything is done, and I'm feeling great from the bike or run, I'll sit down to read. Reading is fun too and I like to find good books. I like to plow through them.

I'll read for a little bit in the afternoon, and pick it up again later at night. It feels so great to read a good book, after accomplishing all that other important stuff. It's a great way to end my day.

And I like that routine so much, that I could do it all day, every day. At least for now.

SECRET TO WEALTH

What if you knew the secret to wealth? Would you use it?

We all dream of money. We dream of fame, fortune, and success. We dream of being happy and peaceful. We want a life full of contentment.

We want to be loved. We want a life of happiness.

And we especially avoid pain – we don't want to be yelled at, or to struggle, or suffer.

But what if these things are wrong. What if the world is lying to you? What if the dreams will lead to misery?

Then what are you supposed to do?

—

I read a book that really messed with my mind: *Think and Grow Rich* by Napoleon Hill. (I'm not linking to it. I don't recommend it.)

The concept of the book is interesting. 80 years ago (literally) Napoleon Hill was commissioned by Andrew Carnegie – one of history's wealthiest men – to find the secret of being rich.

Hill successfully interviewed 500 of the richest men in America to find their secret.

The one common denominator – and the actual "secret" Hill uncovered – was these men believed in themselves. They wholeheartedly believed one day they would be rich.

That's not really much of a secret, but Hill explains it has nothing to do with education or up-bring – just the opposite – it's whatever confidence you've built for yourself and your willingness to succeed at all cost.

—

Think and Grow Rich should be required reading for any businessman. There are plenty of solid anecdotes and interesting tales about great business triumphs of the 20th century. It's very interesting.

The book has been updated for today's generation. New editors have added contemporary stories we're all familiar with, like the rise of Microsoft and McDonald's. It's all compelling and inspiring.

However, *Think and Grow Rich* takes a whack-a-doo turn halfway through. Hill begins to explain the actual method for improving your self-talk.

Hill explains you need to get up every morning and pray to the Money-god. "Money-god" is my terminology and not found in the book, but Hill eloquently shows how you need to recite mantras and prayers of "I will be rich, I will be rich."

"Dear Money-god – I believe I will be rich one day. Please give me success and wealth. Amen."

Yep. That sounds like praying to the Money-god to me.

The problem is, this nonsense actually works.

If you're constantly praying about money, you're going to get it. If your daily thoughts are consumed with being successful, you're going to get it.

But you better be careful what you ask for.

—

One of the most difficult times in my life was when I got what I wanted.

I had always wanted to be a writer. That's all I ever dreamed about – to write and be rich.

I finally found a job that I liked. While not a writing job, per se, it was slow and there was plenty of time to write for myself and to read. It was an awesome job.

But the problem was, it was the night shift, and it was ruining my life.

At the time I didn't know how bad it was. I actually thought everything was great.

For once I looked forward to going to work – something I had always wanted. There was no more dread. It was exciting to be able to write and accomplish my goals. I even went to work on my days off, to use an empty conference room, and write some more.

(Who wants to work on their day off? I mean really…)

And not to mention we were making lots of money. It was the most money we ever had. So life should have been great. I finally figured me and my wife had succeeded, able to chase our dreams and reach our goals.

—

But what's the saying, "I couldn't see the forest for the trees?"

All of a sudden, I was never seeing my wife – our schedules were totally opposite. And forget about attending church – both of us were working on Sunday morning.

Suddenly, everything was a mess and our lives felt like a living hell.

But why? I didn't know.

I blamed a lot of things. I blamed my tiredness. I blamed other people. I blamed her.

It was everyone else's fault except my own.

Because clearly – I was the only one actually "living my dream." Everyone else could suck it.

Realizing how bad things had gotten and how "checked out of life" I had become, I quit that job.

I felt bad. Like I was giving up on my dream, and back to failing all over again.

But honestly, there were a lot of other things that mattered more to me than that job – like my wife and my church. My relationship with Christ.

—

A grey-haired old man once told me, "You can have anything you want in life. But you can't have everything."

It's true. It's like a confusing Yoda quote, but it's very true.

The things we chase will damage us – these goals and dreams – things that stress us out and compel us to action.

But if it's not Christ we're pursuing, we'll end up in a world of hurt.

Paul says in Philippians 4:12, "I know how to live on almost nothing or with everything. I have learned the secret of living in every situation, whether it is with a full stomach or empty, with plenty or little."

Paul knows. He's been there. He's lived in the best of times and the worst. He's been high and low.

And ultimately, he knows this world has nothing to offer us – NOTHING.

The only thing we should be chasing, the only thing we should have our minds focused on, is that of Christ.

Because everything else is a lie.

You can't pray to both God and the Money-god.

You have to decide. And there's only one right choice.

HAPPY LIFE

A happy life is easy to ruin. A recent study from the *Journal of Applied Psychology* revealed being rude to someone early in the morning will affect their mood all day.

No crap. We don't need a scientific study to know getting cut-off in rush hour traffic will ruin our day.

—

This happened to me this morning. Cruising down University Pkwy, I was tailgating very close to the car in front of me when a beat-up '84 Corolla cut me off.

"Dude! There's not even room for you here!"

What a moron.

I was already fighting a melancholy mood, but this guy set me off.

The trouble is, minor infractions like this happen all the time. We drive to work every day and are constantly irritated.

Then we drive home at night, and get irate all over again, just in time to see the Mrs.

What a pleasant experience indeed.

—

There's a coffee shop in France with a creative pricing structure. If you're pleasant to the barista, a cup of coffee will cost $5. If you're rude, it'll cost $10.

There's an instant karma tax for rudeness. How clever.

But why do we need a special tax to remind us to be polite?

Being nice to other people should be our default mode, but it's not.

—

During Christmas rush, we went to the mall, on a Saturday. What a bad idea.

A "gang" of relatives swarmed the parking lot, blocking traffic. They were screaming and yelling at another "gang" of shoppers.

Who knows what they were arguing about, but I'm sure it had to do with a parking spot.

I wanted to watch. I wanted to catch the fight on my smart-phone and send it to TMZ. I was hoping my video would go viral.

But it dissipated as no punches were thrown – sadly. (Someone deserved to be knocked out)

—

The scene in the mall parking lot brought back Post Traumatic Stress for me.

Years ago we were caught in a similar altercation.

We pulled into a parking spot and got out of our car.

A young female driver squealed around the corner, blocked us in, and started yelling at us.

We thought it was a scam like we were being *Punked* and Ashton Kutcher was about to jump out from behind the bushes and yell, "Gotcha." It was clearly a joke.

But she was outraged. Apparently, she had "claimed" the empty parking space in her mind – from a few rows away...

I'm not sure if that's how the parking rules work in America, but whatever.

—

Our entire night was ruined. We were going out for a nice dinner, but now the girl had ruined our entire night. All we could talk about was how crazy she was.

I ended up leaving in the middle of the meal to move my car. I feared we'd find a broken window, punctured tire, or key scratches in the paint.

Thankfully, there was nothing like that, and I moved the car with ease.

But as I rounded the corner, looking for a new spot, the girl had illegally parked in the fire lane. She was sitting there, waiting for her next "victim."

What a psycho.

—

When your internal dialog is off kilter – and suddenly a jerk cuts you off – you react in kind. It's like this psychotic biological defense mechanism, in case people are stealing our food or something.

But part of it is that we've become so indifferent to others around us.

There are so many people in the world, that we can yell at someone and never see them again. There are no consequences. Nothing matters at all.

Who cares.

—

Denmark is ranked as having a high quality of life. There are lots of theories to why this is, and some will joke that it's because they have "low expectations." And maybe that's the case.

But the Danish also do life differently. They have a word in Danish called "hygge." It roughly translates to "cozy and happy." They embrace the winter – look forward to it actually – and find ways to make themselves cozy.

Having a positive attitude about the winter is definitely a plus, especially for such a cold climate.

But the Danish also have tighter communities. They help each other out. They care about their neighbors.

Being bundled snuggly in their homes, enjoying hygge, has its benefits.

They're stuck with the same people – seeing them every day. They can't afford to be rude to each other. They need each other. They help each other.

It's not a nation of 300 million people crashing their cars into each other, never to see that person again.

It's a small knit community of people, joining together, and respecting one another.

If you ask me, it's a better way to do life.

A kinder way.

FALSE ADVERTISING

False advertising is ruining our lives. As humans, we spend an inordinate amount of time lying to each other. We pretend life is amazing, that we are successful, important, and happy.

We want others to think we are living "the good life," while others are missing out.

We want to be loved.

And still, we constantly chase things that will make us happy. We see someone else doing something and we want it.

But this never fixes anything. Nothing ever truly satisfies.

—

If you know me at all, I love donuts. I'm not much of a foodie – I could care less about fancy feasts or overpriced desserts – but when it comes to donuts, I lose my mind.

There's a switch of excitement that flickers in my head. I definitely like the taste – the soft cakey goodness – but it goes deeper than that.

Living in New England, Dunkin' Donuts is everywhere. It's a way of life. Everyone starts their day with a Dunkin' coffee (regular, please). They're on every corner. You can't get away from them if you tried.

—

Growing up, we'd visit my grandparents on Saturday morning. And with the amount of cousins, aunts, and uncles, there was always a revolving door of friendly faces.

And the one regular guest – a box of donuts. Inevitably, someone would arrive toting a dozen Dunkin' Donuts.

I'd look forward to this moment all week. When I could finally get my hands on a chocolate frosting filled donut – one of those white powdered heart attacks stuffed with cake frosting. Yum!

Even now, every time I eat a donut, my mind flies back to Saturday mornings, sitting on my grandparent's carpet.

We'd wait eagerly while Grampy would fling handfuls of change on the floor, then us kids would scatter like maniacs, scuffing our knees collecting the money.

He called it a "Pig Scramble." And after the sugar-rush and all the running around, we'd only leave with $2.57. But to us, it felt like a million bucks.

—

Then later in life, I learned about the "Best Donut in the World."

In the days of the Travel Channel and Food Network, it felt like Voodoo Donuts was the first bakery to go viral. Everyone knew about Voodoo Donuts, even if you'd never been to Oregon.

They had a characteristic donut shaped like a voodoo doll, complete with pretzel stick jammed through the heart. Then remove the "needle" and it would bleed strawberry jam blood. Priceless.

So for New Years, my wife and I visited Portland, Oregon. Already on the West Coast visiting family, we stopped by this hipster-hot-spot for one specific reason: Voodoo Donuts.

—

Our first day in Portland, we passed Voodoo Donuts on the way to the hotel. We saw the mile-long line stretching around the block. Instantly we got excited, realizing we had made a great decision to visit this city.

So the next day we got up early to beat the crowd. We arrived as the shop opened, without another customer in sight. We felt on top of the world, with the entire famous bakery before us, and the delicious smells as the donuts rolled out the kitchen.

We ordered all of them. My wife and I had ordered a dozen donuts, to eat between the two of us. But we also couldn't decide what donut would be best. There was a bacon donut and a Fruit Loop donut – too many confusing decisions to make at 6 o'clock in the morning.

We ran back to the hotel in the cold January wind, a box of donuts under our arm. The reception desk in the hotel cheered us on, seeing we had visited the donut-mecca of Portland. We felt like heroes.

—

Back in our room, we cracked open the box and prepared to eat. There were so many options it was impossible to decide. I went with my gut (obviously) and choose the staple: THE voodoo doll.

I cracked him in half and took a bite.

Umm, not what I expected.

It was fine. I was passable as a donut. But it wasn't delicious.

I literally said, "Dunkin' Donuts is better."

In New England, I could have visited 30 Dunkin' Donuts within 10 miles. You can't get away from them. So why was I compelled to travel across the country to get the "World's Best Donut," when it wasn't?

I was confused. Very confused.

—

Obviously, it was a lie. All a lie.

The Voodoo Donut people have a great business and even smarter marketing campaign. If you're in Portland you must stop by, even just for the Instagram pics.

But if you REALLY want a great donut, go to Blue Star Donuts.

My wife and I were depressed after our Voodoo Donut disaster. We still had a half dozen donuts rotting away that we weren't going to eat.

Then one morning, as we contemplated suicide and ending our lives (because clearly there was nothing else worth living for) we saw a man with a Blue Star Donuts box tucked under his arm. And then we saw a second person. It felt like an invitation from God to keep on living.

We immediately tracked down Blue Star Donuts a few blocks away and were impressed. It was a cleaner place with a trendy feel and the donuts were spectacular. They were flavorful and fluffy – and arguably, the best donuts I've had in my entire life.

I miss Blue Star Donuts a lot.

I wish there was one on every corner.

THE MEDIA LIES

The media lies. Everything you see is a lie. TV, movies, the internet is full of liars.

Everyone is trying to sell you something. They're trying to make money off you, preying off insecurity, and hoping you'll throw money away to fix the problem – the same "fake problem" they've convinced you that you have.

—

I went to New York City once and hated it.

That was quite a surprise. I thought it'd be cool.

Everything I heard made New York seem like the most wonderful place in the world. Like it was full of energy and life and fun.

It was none of that. It was full of noise, tourists, and angry cab drivers.

As soon as I stepped foot on New York soil, I could feel the tension. It was like a panic of energy. Everyone was stressed out and angry. It was a very strange sensation indeed.

—

Wanting to escape the hysteria, I was glad to finally check-in to the hotel. I wanted to hide in my room and relax.

That was, "if" we could ever check-in. We were at a very nice hotel and expected a certain level of service, but there was none. It was the opposite of service.

We were forced to wait, with no explanation or apology. It was the worst hotel service I had ever received.

I looked around to the strangers waiting around me. Who knows where they had come from, or what their stories were, as everyone began to mumble, "Can you believe this? It's New York, I guess."

I said to my wife, "This is just how it's going to be, apparently. We better get used to it." This is the real New York, after all, the one they don't want you to see in the movies. The one where everyone is miserable and treats each other like crap. The one where everyone is stressed out.

New York sucks.

—

As a tourist myself, there were interesting things to see. The World Trade Center is one of them. That at least feels like holy ground. It's a literal cemetery. And it makes my heart break for our county.

But as soon as you're a block away, it's back to throwing elbows and carving your place in the world.

And not to mention the yelling. Why is everyone yelling at each other, about everything? Geez. Relax. But it's like they physically can't. I could feel it too. That pressure to fight. The city takes over your soul.

But this wasn't the New York of my dreams – that countless romantic comedies and gorgeous car commercials make me believe.

New York is horrible. Did I mention it sucks?

—

Social media and bloggers make you think you're missing out. They want you to see images of wonderful places, and make you jealous.

But you need to look past the picture, look past the lie. It's all fluff.

We went to the place with the "frozen hot chocolate." It was gross. It tasted like a packet of hot chocolate in ice water – you could make that at home and dump it down the drain yourself. Yuck.

And the original cronut place. It was a cool bakery, and the cronut was yummy, but it wasn't worth the "out of the way" trip. There are plenty of local bagel places to explore that are just as memorable.

Speaking of bagels, there's one Instagram famous bagel store who makes the "rainbow bagel." I'm sure you've seen it. We didn't go there, and I'm glad we didn't. Some people had commented that it's a below average bagel, and it's only worth going for the picture, and I believe it.

The only reason to get the rainbow bagel is to make other people jealous. WTF?!? What kind of society have we become that our sole mission in life is to chase down Instagram photo ops?

Absolutely ridiculous.

—

Listen, New York sucks. Don't go there.

If you're feeling like you're missing out, you're not. I'm sure there are a million unexplored gems in your city that you never even knew about – places that have no social media marketing campaigns – but are actually pretty amazing.

Go to the beach, explore a park, try out a new sandwich shop. I'm sure you'll be just as satisfied.

I look at all these travel blogs and they promise, "Paris is amazing." "Hawaii is amazing." "Colorado is amazing."

No, they're not. There's nothing special about any of these places. Don't believe the hype. They're all exactly the same as your home town, and if you visit them, you may find they're actually worse.

So don't get your hopes up chasing a lie. There's nothing out there for you – except misery and despair.

Be happy with what you have, and don't shove it in other people's faces – because you really don't know who you're hurting – most of all, yourself.

NEW JOBS

New jobs are hard. We all like to stay in our comfort zone, in the familiar, rather than venture into the harsh unknown.

What if we try something new and fail? How should we respond? Should we get down on ourselves and never try again?

—

I've had lots of jobs. I counted the other day and came up with 21. That's 21 different jobs, all with unique W2's and 1099's for tax purposes, ever since I was 16 years old.

Some of those jobs were short stints, while others were for 3+ years.

But I was analyzing what jobs I liked and grading each accordingly. I came up with some interesting discoveries, for me personally to pursue in the future.

What was most interesting was how I hated most of them – like with belligerent disgust.

—

One of my worst jobs was a camp counselor.

I had never gone to summer camp as a kid. I never wanted to. There were lots of day camps I attended and different soccer style camps, but never an all-out summer variety.

I lived in the country for crying out loud and lived at the lake all summer. Why would I pay extra to have the same experience elsewhere?

But as an adult, I figured, "Hey, I've never been to summer camp. Maybe now will be a good time."

It wasn't. And it will never be.

—

My thought process and risk tolerance were healthy in the beginning. I was becoming comfortable with stretching myself, trying new stuff, going off to college, jumping at internships – and figured summer camp would be a breeze.

It wasn't. I hated it from the start.

To summarize my experience is this: Babysitting. Glorified babysitting.

I never imagined summer camp would be plagued with bickering kids. I figured it would be bonfires, s'mores, and late night cabin raids.

For me, as a 20-year-old, I had finally figured out how to take care of myself and make my own life choices. Now my summer had been reduced to making sure shoes were tied and no one stabbed their eye with a stick.

It was a constant barrage on my senses and mental state. At the end of every day I was glad for the sun to set and the day to be over. I was exhausted.

Suddenly, I had a brand new appreciation for mothers.

—

I was tired and needed a break.

Once a week I had an entire day off. I couldn't wait for that day, because I would wake up early and run out of the cabin. I would get in my car and peel rubber in the gravel driveway. I needed to leave, and relax, before I went totally insane.

All I wanted to do was go home and stare at a wall. I didn't want anyone to talk to me. All I wanted to do was die. And I dreaded every moment of having to return to camp, to babysit some more, and deal with those hooligans.

I was in way over my head. I needed to get out.

—

The end of the summer came with huge relief.

I was excited to get back to college, be around my peers, and read some books – just anything to get away from those kids.

And after camp, all I could think about was how much I hated it. Life had been going right before that, as I was growing and learning new things. But camp slapped me with the silly stick.

I learned not all experiences are created equal. Not all jobs are equal.

I have terrific friends who love camp. I have friends who are great teachers and parents.

And for me, I learned a lot about what doesn't work – sometimes that's valuable.

For whatever reason, I had a burning passion in my gut that I needed to try summer camp. I don't like camping or any outdoors stuff, and felt like I needed to overcome that fear.

Now that I had tried it, and given it my all, I learned a lot about what I'm meant to pursue.

It means I don't need to be working with kids, or a preschool teacher, or any babysitting type roles.

But there are also people who are great at that stuff and love kids.

I saw that too.

—

That summer camp experience taught me a lot.

I still follow my gut. I have things I need to chase. And I try new things with all my effort.

But if things don't go right – and it ends up like summer camp all over again – I don't beat myself up.

I don't tell myself that I'm a failure and good at nothing. I just chalk it up to finding what I'm not good at, and then try again.

Because ultimately, no one even cares that I failed at being a camp counselor. No one even remembers.

No one ever says, "Remember that time you were a camp counselor? You should go back to that. You should try again."

—

In all those 21 different jobs, there are nuggets of what I do like – things that I'm good at and able to pursue.

And finding those passions are worth their weight in gold.

FEEL AMAZING
EVERY DAY

It's easy to feel amazing every day. But it takes effort.

For me, I've relied on these lifesaving tools – the things I need when life feels impossible.

And so you're aware, this section is going to be a bunch of quotes and wisdom from old men. If you don't like catch-phrases and metaphors, move along.

But if you'd like some words of encouragement, then proceed.

—

Lots of times I feel miserable. Life just isn't going right, or the way I expect, and it sucks. It's like a horrible cloud follows me everywhere and my life feels disappointing. Like I'm a failure. And a horrible person. And I should just quit everything and crawl back into bed. (Because sleeping, and avoiding issues, is clearly the appropriate adult response...)

Yet, when I'm in these dark moments, I have clarity. I'm able to recognize what's going on and that I don't have to feel that way. I remember better times, of feeling good, and being optimistic. (like even a month ago)

I begin to realize my thoughts have internalized themselves and all I think about is myself. I don't do this on purpose, but it's an easy trap to fall in. It's like, "I don't feel good, I'm miserable, I want to do something else."

And it's doubly hard when it's the holidays and New Year's rolls around. Everyone is throwing parties and acting all excited. Everyone's motivated with brand new plans and resolutions. It's all about me, me, me – what I want and what I need.

But then wait! I realize I'm miserable and have been for a month. I realize I've been thinking about worldly things and nothing else.

So I literally say to myself, "I'm miserable. Let's break the cycle."

—

A wise old man once asked me, "If you're miserable: Have you been in the Word (the Bible) or helped anyone recently?"

Geez. That strikes like a searing iron through a black heart.

It's painful to hear when you're in a gloomy state. Actually, it's the last thing you want to hear – that it's your own fault you suck at life. But believe me, it's a lifesaver, and the only thing that will bring you out of the pain.

I realize it's true. I realize my morning routines have faltered. I haven't been in the Word. And I literally haven't helped anyone else, well, since never.

Helping people is hard. Reading the Word is hard. It all takes sacrifice and effort.

(It's just easier to do nothing, and feel pity for myself.)

—

Another old man said, "Do the hard thing."

That's obvious advice, but it's hard to follow. Sometimes it's hard to figure out the "thing."

As a financial advisor, I felt miserable a lot. It's a hard job and you're pulled in a million directions. It's hard to figure out what your job actually is.

But after two years (of pain), I finally figured it out: I needed to schedule three appointments every day. That was it. That was my "thing."

I had been taught that since day one, but until you're living in the hurt, you don't appreciate the advice.

If I accomplished that feat, everything would fall into place and life would be easy. If I didn't, life would suck, and it would suck a lot.

—

It seems easy to say, but it's hard to do.

Mark Twain said, "If it's your job to eat a bullfrog, it's best to do it first thing in the morning." (or something similar)

You have to figure out what your bullfrog is, that one thing if you accomplish you'll feel amazing. But if you avoid it and don't eat it, you'll feel gloomy and miserable all day.

As a financial advisor, I remember getting my "thing" done first thing in the morning. Before I read emails or checked the sports scores, I'd gear up and get the task accomplished. It was my sole focus and the thing I needed to do. Nothing else mattered.

After I finished, I could do whatever I wanted with my day. Sure, there'd be real work to do and results from the activity, but if it was a Friday and I wanted to go skiing that afternoon, I would, and I would feel great because I had accomplished my goal.

—

You can find your "thing" too. And you probably don't have to look very far.

You know exactly what it is. It's that thing that's welling inside you and causing a lot of pain.

Admit what it is. Rip it like a band-aid. Start committing to your thing and getting it done every day.

Maybe it's hard, but who cares. If it's something that's important to you, it probably is difficult. It probably takes some sacrifice and extra effort. Maybe it means a new routine. Maybe it means less sleep.

But once you get it done, you'll feel so much better – and then you can go skiing.

Then tomorrow, you can do it all over again. And feel amazing every time.

HARD TASKS

Hard tasks are difficult. Our jobs are tough. Our bosses can be overly demanding.

We work long hours and are exhausted at the end of the day. Sometimes there are things we don't want to do.

So how are you supposed to handle hard tasks – when there's something you don't want to do?

—

For me, interning for Disney was the experience of a lifetime. I got to see the inner-workings of one of the world's best companies.

Doubly too, I got trained in how to be a customer service ninja.

As most guests can attest, one of the primary draws of the Disney Experience is the premier level of customer service.

It seems like every employee is happy, willing, and ready to serve.

And it's because they are.

—

I worked in retail. Generally retail sucks (like Walmart and Target retail is a nightmare). But Disney retail is on another level.

First, they trained me how to properly "count money back." This is an ancient way of returning someone's change.

If the total came out to $12.43, and someone gave you a $20, you'd have to count up from $12.43 to return their change.

It sounds more complicated than it is, and during training it felt daunting, but after practicing, it became second nature, more accurate, and a brilliant customer service technique.

Also, Disney has these cash registers from the 1970s that don't work properly. A normal cash register should calculate the correct change automatically, but Disney doesn't do that.

It's entirely up to you to calculate it in your head – which if you suck at math, can make for some stressful situations.

—

For the $12.43 example, you'd collect the change to get to the nearest dollar. So 57 cents. Then you'd hand this back to the customer and say, "57 cents makes $13."

Then get the rest of the bills and hand those back, counting up the entire way. You'd say, "And two dollars makes fifteen, and five makes 20."

This technique totally perplexes every guest who experiences it. Because no other company does it this way. It's confusing.

The best way to do it, without scaring a guest, is to do it fast and natural. To be quick about it.

But many times I would first hand the change back (counting to $13) and the guest would interrupt and say, "But I gave you a $20."

You'd simply smile, say "Yes," and continue counting back as if you weren't interrupted. They'd figure it out eventually.

—

Nearly once a week too, guests would forget the amount they had given me.

Joe Shaughnessy

When they handed me the $20 bill, I would lay in on the register's dash – NOT putting it in the drawer. I would then proceed to count the change back to $20 and hand it to the customer.

Inevitably, someone would respond, "But I gave you a $50."

Oh man! Talk about a heart-stopping moment for a cashier.

You know you're right and the customer is wrong, but how are you supposed to disagree? Or you could admit you made a mistake and just give them the amount they asked for – but then you'd be stealing from your employer.

Not with the Disney way!

If the customer thought he gave me a $50, I would simply smile (always smile) and say, "Sorry sir, you gave me a $20. I haven't put it in the drawer yet." And show him the bill still sitting on your dash.

Absolutely brilliant. And the best argument avoidance system I had ever seen.

—

The Disney way of counting change is about politeness and putting the customer first.

I would never count change this way on my own. No one would. It takes too much work.

But after all, Disney is in the "customer experience" business and had determined this is the best way to count money back.

I know it worked to save many arguments, always assuring the guest received the exact right amount they deserved.

Disney isn't asking its employees to behave in strange ways for the heck of it – they're doing it because it's the best way – the most magical way.

And it makes a lot of cents.

(See what I did there... I said "cents" instead of "sense." Ha!)

FEAR AT WORK

Fear at work is a real thing. When I interned for Disney, they trained me to do a lot of strange and unnatural things.

One of them was to say, "Come back again and see us real soon."

Come again? What does that even mean?

As a cashier, the managers would grade us on a 10-point scale. Lots of the points were easy to earn, like saying "Hi" and counting back the correct change.

But the one that hung me up, was the "ask them back." I always got a zero.

—

I hated that thing. Asking someone to come back and visit again is such an unnatural ask.

I just assumed skip it and get a 90% on the evaluation.

But for Disney, anything short of perfection is a fail.

After a few months of skating by, an ultimatum came down from the Corporate Mouse:

"Any cast member failing to achieve 100% on their evaluations will be terminated."

There was an official memo, with a lot more magical Disney-speak, but that's effectively what it said.

Ouch.

—

I was worried.

I didn't want to say that dumb thing – it felt so awkward and stupid.

But I was also earning a grade for college credit, so I really did need an A. And I also couldn't afford to get fired – getting an F on an internship wouldn't look good on my permanent record either.

So I had to figure out how to make this work.

I gave it a shot. And failed miserably.

After wrapping up a guest's purchase, I smiled and said, "Come back again and see us real soon?"

After working there for months I had never uttered this ridiculous phrase. It felt like sandpaper on my tongue.

The lady looked at me like I had a virus and scurried away – she didn't want to catch my disease.

I needed to escape. This all felt foreign and wrong.

—

On a day off I wandered around the park. I was miserable, thinking about getting fired.

After a horrible day of banging my brain around the triple-mountain-coasters (Space, Thunder, and Splash), I was startled by hearing a familiar phrase.

As I exited Splash Mountain, an unfamiliar cast member greeted me by saying, "Come back and see us real soon!"

She caught me off guard. She had said it with such excitement and enthusiasm. And it felt natural. Like she really wanted me to ride the ride all over again, soaking my pants once more.

I wished I could have been in her position. I was jealous. It felt so easy and natural to say "bye" to people as they left an attraction.

I worked in retail after all. That was such a strange place to ask someone to come back and buy more stuff. It felt insincere.

—

Now more depressed than ever, I needed to eat.

The only decent place to eat in Frontier Land is the turkey leg stand. It's a big greasy hunk of meat, but it's delicious and tastes like ham. So it's awesome.

As I paid and received my order, the kind man said, "Thanks and come again."

Now I was hearing this phrase everywhere – it's like when you need a new car and you swear every TV commercial is directed at selling you a new car.

He said it so naturally and with such ease. And it felt like he cheated. He hacked the phrase down, cutting it to bits, but the essence was there. I was impressed.

—

With this newfound revelation, I was excited to return to work.

After ringing up the first guest of the day, I was ready and eager to utter my new catchphrase, as I said, "Thanks and come again."

I said it as naturally as you'd say, "How's it going?" It's a phrase that doesn't need acknowledgment. It's meaningless and no one takes you literally.

I had found my trick and it stuck.

As the next round of evaluations came, I was happy and excited for my manager to rate me.

I had figured it out. I had solved the difficult puzzle.

So when the time came, I ticked all the boxes and got everything right. For the first time, I finally received a 100% on my evaluation.

I was so excited I could squeal.

It meant I could keep my job and was on my way to successfully pass the internship.

And it meant I was finally the perfect Disney cast member – everything Walt had ever dreamed.

YOUR GIFT

Your gift isn't special. Newsflash: No one else is better than you.

Everyone is exactly equal. No one has any special gift or talent that you can't get too.

So stop lying to yourself, thinking you can't be successful.

Because you can. And I'll show you how.

—

Growing up, I looked at writers like having a superpower. I read science fiction books by Robert A. Heinlein and was blown away.

I couldn't understand how he did it – I figured he was a magician.

I had no idea how a person could write in such a way that would transport the reader to another world. I figured he was like the smartest man ever and had doctorate degrees, with years of higher education – a bunch of unattainable stuff – like a special gift.

And I had read a bunch of books from different authors and multiple genres. Nothing caught my interest. Reading was boring and it sucked. I just thought I wasn't a good reader.

That was, until, I fell in love with science fiction. And my world changed.

—

Joe Shaughnessy

I read science fiction all the time. I'd sit in bed and read a chapter before falling asleep. I couldn't stop reading.

And my teachers wanted me to quit.

They said, "It's great that he's reading, but he really needs to read something besides science fiction." (Because it'll rot his brain or something…)

My mom nearly had a heart attack.

She had just gotten me to become an avid reader, after spending endless summers at the library and countless trips to Barnes and Noble.

Reading was boring. I hated it. It felt like torture.

She knew I wasn't stupid, but she couldn't get me to sit still long enough to read.

And it wasn't my mom's fault or my teacher's fault.

It was the book's fault. It was the writer's fault.

Because every book sucked.

—

Even now, as an adult, this mantra is still true: Reading can be excruciatingly boring.

I pick up lots of books, hoping they'll catch my interest and pull me in.

Most of them don't.

I have a rule, that after 50 pages, if the book isn't interesting, I quit. I toss it. Because I've read plenty of books all the way through and they never get better.

So if the author doesn't know how to pull you in by page 50, do you think it'll get better by page 400? Nope.

So chuck it. And move on with your life. Find something else that interests you.

—

I have no idea how to raise kids, but I'm very thankful for my mom's wisdom. She exposed me to a lot of different things – like sports and music, science and math.

There are plenty of kids who know they "want to be" a doctor, or a baseball player, or a missionary, or a photographer. And good for them.

It's probably a relief to know what you want to be at such a young age. It takes the mystery and guesswork out of things.

But what if you don't know? What are you supposed to do?

It can be confusing, to be sure.

—

Malcolm Gladwell talks about the 10,000 hours it takes to become a master. He evaluated many professionals in their field and discovered the one common denominator was the time commitment these people invested in their craft.

No matter the job, all these people had invested thousands of hours, perfecting their skills.

At Golf: Tiger Woods – 10,000 hours.

At Football: Tom Brady – 10,000 hours.

At Writing: Stephen King – 10,000 hours.

These are all masters in their profession and are very good at what they do.

However, please understand this: You don't have to spend thousands of hours to get a job – to be a true master you do – but not to be "in the game."

—

I've spent a lot of time learning new things – it feels like the more you learn, you realize the less you know.

As an 18-year-old kid, I felt like I knew everything (what teenager doesn't?).

But after 4 years of college, learning about business and computers, I realized I had no practical skills, was unemployable, and at the bottom of a huge career ladder. There were more brilliant employees ahead of me, all with more knowledge and experience. I had a lot to learn.

Then after 7 years in the financial world, studying hard for major exams, and deep diving into specific roles, I learned I was merely adequate at my job. There were still others beyond me with long corporate careers and a lifetime of experience.

Now, after 7 years of fiction writing, I'm still a rookie. I'm getting my foot in the door, establishing myself, but I still have an entire career ahead of me. I've committed roughly 1,800 hours to fiction writing, which doesn't include extracurricular skills like full time writing jobs, reading, or nonsensical years of journaling or joke writing.

—

Honestly, it was difficult for me to find the writing path, and I'm just barely getting my footing.

But what clicked for me was the 10,000 hour concept.

I figured if I ever wanted to master anything, I would need to invest those hours. But I couldn't bear to spend the time on something I hated.

If I wanted to be a master, I needed to find something I enjoyed.

I finally found writing. It's something I love and gives me peace every day.

I think you can find something too. Just understand there's

nothing intrinsically special about Tiger Woods or Tom Brady. They're gifted at what they do, but only because they put in the time.

So try something new, chase a thing you're passionate about and that makes you happy.

Because if you're ever going to be good at something, you're going to have to spend your life doing it.

BE KIND ALWAYS

You should always be kind. You never know who you'll help.

There's a bike trail in Florida where everyone is rude. No one says hi to each other or waves.

The daily troubles of the world have followed these people to the path, where they continue to fight and scratch their way along.

It's a dog-eat-dog world and the path is no different.

But this is not how a bike path should be.

The path should be kind.

—

I've ridden all sorts of trails.

State parks and trails built by mountain bikers have this community feel. There are conversations being had, general pleasantries exchanged, and an overall positive mood.

Even in New England – which is full of grumpy people – the bike trails are full of dog walkers and horseback riders, all waving at each other, acknowledging each other's existence, and available for a quick smile.

It's nice out there, and you feel welcome, in the woods of New England.

—

The Florida trail is in the city, and it feels like you're constantly being cut off.

I've seen cars blow stop signs, other bikers zooming around pedestrians never announcing their presence. There are homeless people flagging you down.

It's just not a nice feeling. It feels like more anxiety and stress – all the stuff you're supposed to be avoiding out on the trail.

—

One time, another biker shouted at me, and I didn't know what to do.

I thought he wanted to rob me. Because no one talks to each other, these are the rules. And he had been the first to break the silence. Obviously, this wasn't going to end well.

He shouted, "Do you have a wrench?"

What? I didn't understand what he said. I thought he wanted money. It didn't register in my mind what he needed.

But he was old and looked foreign. At the very least I could keep my distance and zoom away on my bike if need be.

There was no one else around – no hooligans in the bushes – so I wasn't about to be jumped. It didn't feel like a trick.

It was such a strange encounter, that I decided he actually needed help.

—

When I'm at a traffic intersection and stopped at a red light, there's a way to properly position the pedal on your right leg, like a sprinter ready to burst from the starting line. You immediately push off and gain instant momentum.

As I stopped to help this man, I "loaded" my pedal, ready to burst away if trouble came.

"My brakes are loose," he said. "I need to tighten them."

Oh, thank God, I thought. I didn't need to tackle him after all.

He continued to explain he had just bought the bike from Walmart and was enjoying the first test drive. But being Walmart, they assembled the bike wrong, obviously.

"I don't carry tools with me," I said. I'm usually never far from home. If I blow a tire I'm more likely to ditch the bike and walk back.

But I wanted to help the man. Could I fix a brake with my bare hands? Nope.

"There are bike stations along this path," I explained. "They have air pumps and tools."

—

He was beyond thankful.

He launched into his life story, how he had just moved here from Poland.

I asked if he knew my Polish friends. He didn't. But like so many other Europeans in Florida, there's a huge community of Polish here.

He continued talking, into a longer conversation, about his daughter and his troubles getting settled in. About wanting to ride a bike again, like he had back home. And mostly about how Walmart sucks, which I could appreciate.

I cared for a moment, but I really needed to leave. I wanted to get home and eat dinner.

Besides, he didn't understand the rules of the road: No one was supposed to talk to each other.

He was new. He didn't know.

But because he had broken the silence, it felt foreign and strange.

—

I'm on a new path now.

I'm out running and exercising – trying to feel better and get the cobwebs out of my head.

And once again, no one says hi. No one waves. It's the same rude nightmare all over again.

So I'm changing that.

I'm waving as I pass, I'm saying hi to people. I'm refusing to let sadness win.

I want to spread joy and get a new trend going.

Because all I ever think about is that foreign man. How we're all from somewhere and we all have a story to tell.

And sometimes too, the brakes are broken and the wheels of life are falling apart.

All we need is someone to stop, to help us, and get us back on the right path again.

RESOLUTION FAIL

Did your New Year's Resolution fail? What happens in February, have you already quit? I bet you have.

You dummy. You've become a statistic, but it's not your fault.

New Year's Resolutions always fail.

—

I failed too. I couldn't manage to keep my Resolution.

But my Resolution was this: "To Make No Resolutions."

I'm tired of always chasing impossible dreams. I'm always getting hurt and failing and suffering.

I just wanted a year with nothing to do. To chase nothing. And to have no motivation.

I wanted a year of peace, complacency, and to be satisfied.

I wanted a year to be happy with what I have.

Then I failed. I made it a week – to January 5th – that's longer than I thought I'd last.

By Friday I was back to my rainmaker ways, trying to take over the world, and crush everything in my path.

I was already making plans on doing This, That, and The Other Thing. All these other plans that would flip my world on its head.

And I felt bad about it. I failed – because I can't sit still.

—

If you want to change your life, DO NOT do it on New Year's Day.

This is a recipe for disaster. You're going to fail. You're joining a group of other failures who can't make changes in their life during the normal year.

It's statistics. It's labels.

Don't put yourself in that group. Decide to be different, to do it on your own terms. You don't want to be defined with a group of people who can't make habits stick.

You need to join the people who do. Who succeed. And who find a way.

Successful people are making other plans – throughout the entire year, on a daily and weekly basis – regardless of the arbitrary "New Year's Resolution."

New Year's Resolutions suck. Avoid them at all cost. It'll just make you feel worse about yourself than you already do.

—

As a kid, I learned a new skill.

There's a trick in soccer called a "rainbow." The ball is placed at your feet, then rolled behind you, and kicked over your head with your heel. It flies over you in a rainbow arc. The ball then lands in front of you.

It's a beautiful move when executed properly. When it's wrong, it looks horrible, and the ball goes flying everywhere.

A rainbow too is totally pointless. It's not effective in a game.

Regardless, even though I was a mediocre soccer player, I was determined to add a rainbow to my arsenal.

During one long weekend of watching my sister's soccer tournament, I was bored out of my mind. I decided it would be fun to practice the rainbow technique.

I sucked. I kept kicking that ball everywhere. It was really hard.

But day after day, I stuck to it. I just kept dribbling and flipping that ball over my head.

Finally, by the end of the weekend, I had figured it out.

I managed to feel the ball roll across my calf, and the proper jumping technique to kick the ball simultaneously.

It was awesome. I felt such joy and relief. I had succeeded.

And I didn't need a New Year's Resolution to do it. I knew it could be done, I had seen professionals do it, and was determined to figure it out.

—

The brilliant podcast This American Life ran a story on the dichotomy between a "rich" private high school and a "poor" public high school.

It's shocking, to say the least, to see the polarity between the "have" and "have-nots."

Regardless of what camp you're in, we all get blinded by own sphere of influence – our bubble – the people we surround ourselves with. We subscribe to the doctrines and beliefs of the life-path set before us.

It's not that the rich kids are inherently smarter – because they're not. I've met plenty of idiotic rich people. And it's certainly not the case that poor kids are dumb – that's wrong in so many ways.

But when your entire culture is pounding you and insisting you will succeed, by going to college and beyond – you have no choice but to follow suit – even if you're a moron.

And likewise, when your community is failing you, and no one believes in you, you will automatically default and fall in line –

even if you're the smartest person in the room.

Why should you bother to try? You're just going to be a dish-washer anyway.

What a horrible lesson to teach our children.

We should all be ashamed of ourselves.

—

But we're not ashamed. We can't see what we're doing – it's a blind spot.

We're living our lives exactly as we've been taught, and no different.

So when it comes for goal setting, what group are you in?

Are you with the New Year's Resolutionists who set yearly goals and inevitably fail?

Or are you with the Dreamers, who understand no one else is smarter than you or more talented? We're all exactly equal and it's only our mindset that sets us apart.

You know exactly what "school" you're in. You just have to admit it – if you ever want to break through.

DON'T BE LAZY

Being lazy is easy. It's fun to sit around and relax.

On the flip-side, routines are hard. Deciding to commit to something new, to change your life is hard.

None of this is simple. No one ever said it would be.

—

The other day someone commented on how I "like routines." That struck me as odd. I haven't always been that way.

Yes, currently, it seems like I'm always chasing something, writing every day, forming good habits and morning routines.

Habits have become an important aspect of my life. Habits make me feel good.

I don't much like surprises. I like to plan my day and have a sense of what's important and needs to be accomplished.

But it's not like I came out of the womb as a "routine master" or "habit ninja."

Quite the opposite: I'm lazy.

—

My favorite pastime is watching TV. I can spend countless hours in front of the boob-tube watching whatever program catches my fancy.

Whether that's sports, reality shows, house-flipping programs, cooking specials, talk shows, or entertainment news – it's all compelling and interesting.

TV sucks me in. I can sit there for days (yes, days) just watching TV as life outside passes by.

But growing up, we didn't have TV. It wasn't until middle school that we finally got cable TV (how we survived before that, I'll never know).

And once cable TV was in the house, I was like a moth to the flame. I couldn't look away no matter how hard I tried.

Saturday mornings were the worst. There were a million amazing cartoon shows to watch. I'd gobble them up as fast as I could because inevitably there were chores to do or sports games to play.

I never wanted to go. I threw a fit every time. All I wanted was to sit on my comfy couch and watch the *X-Men*.

—

As an adult, I'm fully aware of this addiction. I try to be careful and take it in tiny doses.

Yet sometimes, an entire Saturday will pass, and all I've managed to do was watch TV all day.

At the moment it feels good – it feels refreshing. But over the long-haul, I'm not doing myself any favors.

Ultimately, I'm not accomplishing anything. I'm being lazy. Life is just passing by, again.

—

Recently, I had to make a hard sacrifice. I had to cut out TV.

After work, I'm exhausted. Work is hard. It's been a long day. Everyone should be tired. That's what work is. It's work.

I come home and plop on the couch. All I wanted to do was

relax, watch my favorite TV shows, and follow the adventures of my YouTube friends.

It's fun, and something I looked forward to each day – the highlight, after a difficult weekday.

Yet in the midst of that pleasure, life was out of whack. I didn't feel good, my goals were off the rails, and I generally felt unhealthy.

There were important things I wanted to accomplish, which weren't getting done. There were excuses, it'd be easier in the future, under different circumstances, when things changed.

—

Inevitably, I realized this 2-hour time block after work was ruining my life.

I had a choice to make. I could continue watching TV, which I would enjoy at the moment, but the rest of my week would suck.

Or, I could sacrifice that 2-hour block and do something constructive – I could run and exercise, get off my butt and move around. And then I could write, to make time for what really mattered.

So that's what I did.

Now, after work, I immediately rush into the house and change into workout gear. I'm exhausted – I can feel it creeping up on me. If I listen to my body, I'm going to immediately crash on the couch and relax – because that's what I deserve and need.

Instead, I rush outside and start running. As soon as I do I feel great. I'm outside, which is nice and listening to a podcast. Running isn't so bad when you can find ways to enjoy it.

Then after, I find a quiet place and write. I work on my goals and aspirations. It feels amazing when you're able to accomplish difficult things.

And then I'm done. I allow myself to finally relax.

I still get some TV to watch, but it's much less than before, and I feel a whole lot better watching it now.

—

So I have a choice to make.

I can either watch TV and enjoy the temporary pleasure. But the rest of my week will suck and I'll feel miserable.

Or, I can do something difficult and exercise. At the moment it feels hard and painful to choose the difficult option. But after doing it, I feel so much better all week long.

MAKE FRIENDS

As an adult, making friends is hard. It suddenly seems like everyone is too busy to add more friends to their life – like somehow a new person, means a new commitment, and extra effort.

Like we're all sucked for time and energy, and the last thing we want is to spend energy on someone we don't know, or who won't return the favor.

Making friends is hard, but it doesn't have to be that way.

—

As an 18-year-old, going off to college for the first time, I was determined to make friends.

I think everyone is. Suddenly, you're ripped from your family and everyone you've known your entire life, and forced to start from scratch, with these strange people you've just met.

But the thing is, everyone feels that way. Everyone needs friends and is looking to be accepted.

I got really lucky with my group of friends and am thankful for them. The people I met in that first week of school remained my close friends for the next four years. It was a pretty awesome connection to have.

Granted, throughout the years, there would be new people to enter our clique – it wasn't like we were exclusive – but the same core remained the same.

And as you familiarize yourself with a college campus, you begin to see the groups of people that belong together. They're always hanging out and doing life together.

College kids have a knack for making friends and building new support systems. It's like they're rebuilding the family they lost to begin with.

However, once we graduate and move on with life, it feels like this friend-making muscle wanes.

Suddenly, as adults, we barely have room for anyone other than ourselves.

—

I don't know if this is good or bad – it's just how it is – it feels like adults can only manage 3-4 close relationships, and that's it. Everyone else is closed off. Goodbye.

Life gets in the way. Jobs get in the way. Our dreams and aspirations take a front seat. How does anyone have time for friends when there are schedules to maintain, errands to run, bills to pay, houses to clean, cars to fix, mouths to feed, beds to be made, habits to form, workouts to do, and careers to pursue? Don't get me started on careers...

In college, you have none of that. You go to class, then have nothing to do. You sit around and stare at your friends all week because you're living with them. It's like a friend-making paradise.

—

After graduating from college, there was a hole in my heart. I was missing my friends and the relationships I had formed. I realized I was never getting that experience back. It was a one-time shot. And now it was over. Done.

So I decided to do something about it and tried to make friends again.

I put my career aspirations on the back burner and figured I'd focus on meeting people and making friends once more.

The trouble was, I didn't know how to do it. How do you make friends?

College had been easy – you're all in the same boat. But how do you do it in the real world, when everyone is busy and will easily disregard your unwanted advances? (that sounds creepy and gross, but there's a similarity to making friends as there is dating – it's a 2-way street)

My mind flew back to people who had been nice to me – people I had wanted to be friends with, but couldn't.

These were confident kids in high school. Cool people, presumably, who seemed to have their act together – which no one really does in high school. High school sucks and it's weird.

But what mattered to me, were the people who treated me well. They would say hi to me, no matter what.

And these weren't deep friendships – just nice acquaintances in passing.

—

As I headed into the real world, seeking friends, I took that advice.

I was learning people's names, and saying hi to them, no matter what. I'd entertain conversations and care about the other person.

And even though I desperately wanted to make friends, I pretended like I didn't. I pretended like I was "cool" and had my act together. Even though deep inside I secretly wanted friendships in return.

But then, once people started getting close and thought I was cool, I'd spring the trap, and be like, "Ha! I want to be friends with you too." And they'd be like, "Whoa, cool."

So that's how I made friends again, like a Venus flytrap luring them in.

In that season, I was able to develop my strongest friendships – my wife included – an unintended by-product on my friend-making journey.

But now that I'm older, and have moved on, I'm constantly wondering why it's so hard to make friends again?

I guess I'll never learn.

DEATH AND ADDICTION

A Chinese man died in an internet café. Reportedly, he collapsed after gaming for 3 days straight without food or water.

That story hurts my heart.

I don't understand much of the Asian culture or this new phenomenon of gaming addiction. But one thing is universally clear:

Addiction leads to death.

—

What sort of damage are you doing, to pursue something so earnestly, you're willing to put your own health, sanity, and life on the line?

It must be a passionate pursuit, something deep in your soul, where you're able to block out all other noise and chase after exactly what you want.

It's a commitment – a passion – to go 72 hours without food or water, and have no regard for the consequences.

What could ever be so compelling?

—

This is a fast of the evilest sort. It is a fast of internal motivations and internal struggles. It is an unwavering commitment to pursue your own wants, your own desires, and your own will.

And it is something that will get you killed.

Any time we focus on ourselves, it is a path that leads to destruction and despair.

However, fasting, and the removal of food, is supposed to be good.

As Christian believers, when we talk about fasting, we talk about giving something up and focusing our attention back on Christ – things above ourselves.

A fast is inherently good, it is a positive experience. It's an acknowledgment to get outside yourself, and your addictions, and your hurts, and struggles.

A fast is not supposed to get you killed. A fast will bring you new life.

—

Right now, my wrist and back are killing me.

I sit in the same position all day and forget to move around. I'm focused on writing, editing, and researching.

I get so focused and so involved in my projects that it's hurting me.

So then hours later I take a step back as lightning shoots through my elbow. It feels like I've been beaned by an MLB fastball, and think, "Ow! Geez, I'm a moron."

These activities aren't energizing me – they're bringing me pain and suffering – and in the moment I'm so excited, so invested, and so high on the activity – that I forget how much it will hurt in the end.

—

I've talked about my TV addiction – it's dumb, I know. It's like white people problems, right?

But TV is enjoyable. I like it a lot.

I go to work. And when I come home I watch endless hours of TV. Then I go to bed – rinse and repeat the same routine all week long.

That's not much of a life. That's not a life worth living – that's boring at best.

My recent "fast" is to remove the endless TV watching – I still get an hour to brush up on something fun and worth watching – but the endless marathons have been removed.

There needs to be a healthy balance in everything we do.

And I feel better for it.

—

If you're not careful, a serious addiction can ruin anyone's life.

But there are subtle ones that sneak up on us too: social media, video games, food, work. The list is endless and we all have our weird problems.

But where does it end?

Are you willing to watch 3 days of endless television, without food and water, in an attempt to fill a void, or because you deserve it?

At what point does an addiction become all-consuming, that it'll sneak up on you, and take over your entire existence and you never saw it coming?

Because frankly, the addiction may kill you, and you wouldn't even know.

WRITE A BOOK

Everyone wants to write a book.

Why?

A recent statistic found 3 out of 5 people wanted to write a book at some point in their life.

That's a staggeringly huge number. There are over 7 billion people in the world – that means 4.2 billion want to write a book.

Do we even have room for that many books?

Nope.

—

There's a new podcast called "Launch." It's by screenwriter John August, who's written some interesting films like *Big Fish*, and *Charlie and the Chocolate Factory.*

The podcast is compelling. It's edge-of-your-seat type stuff, with a behind the scenes look at the publishing industry. It's great.

But what's interesting is August wants to write a book. And not just any book, but like a famous book – the next *Harry Potter* level of a book.

Don't we all want to write the next *Harry Potter*? That seems as moronic as saying "we want to win the lottery."

No kidding.

So why can't August be content with his day job, writing movies? He has a great job, a brilliant catalog of films, and a steady paycheck.

Why does he have to write a book?

—

Granted, it's not like everyone wants a writing career – but just the privilege to let their story be heard.

It seems strange that writing is a career anyway – and a bizarrely difficult one at that.

It would be like saying 3 out of 5 people want to perform surgery at some point and be a doctor for a day.

What are you even talking about? What kind of insane dream is that? No one would ever aspire to be a doctor for a day.

So why books?

—

There's something universally uniting about books. Across the globe, it's the one common denominator we have as a species. Whatever tribe, language, or tongue you speak – inevitably there are books written and stories being told.

Even from a young age, it's how we learn. It's how we understand the difference between good and evil.

"Let me tell you a story about a person who did something good – you should aspire to do the same."

Or, "Let me tell you a different story about something bad – don't be like that."

Stories allow us to skip steps.

Instead of learning the stove is hot by touching it (which is a painful lesson, every time) – we're able to avoid pain by other's experiences or learn positive truths from their triumphs.

—

And books – these stories – have lasted for millennia.

All our ancient knowledge is in books. There are tons of religious texts, which have survived the test of time. And even secular books like Homer and the *Iliad*.

These are all incredibly helpful stories, which still resonate and leave a lasting impression today.

When I think about the Bible too – it's people like Paul, the Gospel writers, and even King David in the old testament – these are influential thinkers who are long dead, but their lives and thoughts live with us today.

That's why no one wants to "play doctor for a day." No one remembers who did surgery on your heart.

But everyone remembers who pierced your soul.

—

These authors – these life lessons – have affected us all.

These writers have been lifted onto a strange pedestal as being "the best" or the "most remembered" or the "favorite."

It's like everyone knows how important the authors are in their lives, that one day they too have a story to tell, people to help, and lives to shape.

—

I have them too.

People like Donald Miller and *Blue Like Jazz* have a milestone in my heart.

Growing up and what it means to be a Christian in a world that attacks your beliefs, I found comfort in Miller's journey. He said it's ok to not have the answers and to never really understand the complexity of God – but that He exists, and we can find comfort and beauty there.

I read it in college, and there's plenty of other people like me who loved it. It's defined our generation.

I think of Blue Like Jazz fondly. I wonder what Miller is up to and if he's written any more groundbreaking books.

Look him up. There are other stories, but he's ventured away from full time writing – into running a marketing company.

His company is great and he's helping people in new and interesting ways.

But it's not the same.

It's not books.

—

He answered a question about why he doesn't write books anymore.

His answer: Because he's grown.

He's a different person today than the struggling and desperate person in his 20s. I can respect that. It's a solid answer, and I'm proud of his accomplishments and living a better life. We all want a better life.

Maybe his writing hurts him, and I would never want him to suffer more, just because I want to read more of his books – that's selfish of me.

But what's missing is the underlying nature of the question. The question is this:

"We all aspire to be famous authors and you've reached the summit and changed people's lives. Why aren't you still living there? Why aren't your words resonating through the generations and ripping through people's souls?"

Because we all want to be like those great thinkers, and to have our voice be heard. And to have our thoughts last for thousands of years.

I'm not faulting Donald Miller – he can do whatever he wants.

It's just no one on the outside understands. It's like you've achieved a pinnacle of human accomplishment, diving into the psyche of a generation, and now you want to quit?

It's like you don't want to be Shakespeare anymore. Or if Paul was tired of writing from prison.

Where would our society be if those authors stopped writing? If they no longer felt compelled.

No one gets it. No one understands.

Because everyone wants to write a book.

IDEAS

We all get crazy ideas.

It may seem like a normal melancholy day, as you sit there, minding your own business, sipping coffee and wasting time on the internet – when BAM! – the most brilliant idea you've ever had flies into your skull.

It's like THE answer you've been waiting for. It's that brand new idea, that business venture, or side-hustle you've been waiting for all along.

But then, as the hours pass, you talk yourself out of it. You find a list of "cons" to why you can't pursue this new idea.

And you go back to your pathetic life, depressed at your lack of ambition, and stare aimlessly into the abyss of the internet – praying it will swallow your soul.

—

How do these ideas come into our head, and what should we do with them?

Seriously, why does this happen?

Everyone gets ideas, some good, some bad. And why are we compelled to pursue certain ones?

The other day I nearly applied as an editor for a national maga-zine. I was like, "This is the perfect job" I'll get to edit all day, hang out with writers, and be in my element. This is a life-chan-ging idea.

Then I talked myself out of it.

For one, I'd have to move. Second, I'm not qualified. And third, I actually don't like to edit.

Maybe you can tell – and hopefully you can't – but I manage to work in such a way to do minimal editing. I hate editing.

Why did I ever think I would be a good editor? I'd be an awful editor.

Editing sucks.

—

When I write something horrible, and I hate it, I chuck it.

I say it's a practice piece and I set it aside, to hide in a drawer, never to see the light of day again.

I have hundreds of practice pieces, hundreds of thousands of words. A million words. More than enough to fill multiple volumes of books.

Why? I don't know.

I'm insane is the best answer.

But I'm also practicing my craft, having fun, and enjoying myself. It's just fun.

And the bigger answer too, is I hate editing.

If a writing sample is bad, there's no saving it. I'm not going to spend endless months trying to fix it, only to get nowhere, and have lost all that precious time I could have been writing.

That's not fun.

If it's not fun, I don't want to do it – especially in my free time – when there are other distracting options pulling me away (like YouTube).

—

And another problem is I'm terrible at rules.

Not like grammar and spelling – but like I have an affinity for writing how I think – using waaaay too many em-dashes – – – – and using commas, in, the, wrong, place, just, for, fun, even, though, I, know, it's, wrong.

I can breeze through an article, looking for mistakes and edits – but I hardly care. I like how individual writers write. I like their unique style. It's like a fingerprint for who they are and what they have to say. It's like a view into their soul.

It's their voice.

—

I follow Ann Voskamp.

She's a best-selling Christian author with a deep heart for God. Her journey is spectacular.

I hate to raise someone on a pedestal and be like "This is how a Christian woman should be." But like seriously, this is how a Christian anyone (man or woman) should be.

What I love most about Ann is her complex style of writing.

If you read a paragraph it's not entirely clear what she said or where she's headed. It's like how most women must feel and think, with a million thoughts jumbled around in their mind. Her writing jumps around like that.

It's confusing.

But if you go into her writing, knowing she's speaking from her soul, and these are her deepest, darkest thoughts – then it's a lovely view into a Jesus-seeking heart.

To Ann, this is personal. And it's art.

—

I'm sure Ann gets lots of crap.

Even in the midst of her thousands of supporters and readers, there's gotta be a bunch of haters.

It's hard to read her writing. It's like reading poetry – it's not for everyone.

I can only imagine the first manuscript she sent out for publishing. An editor must have been thinking, "What is this nightmare?" – reject.

What if Ann had listened to those naysayers – that she can't write?

Sadly, we'd be missing her wisdom. All the ladies (and men?) she's helping, would have a gaping hole in their life. And that's not good.

It doesn't matter if you can't write. It doesn't matter if you can't run a business. It doesn't matter if you're not qualified, or not good enough, or allow the opinions of others to rule your life.

If you're not following your ideas and pursuing what matters to you, then you're not living the life God created for you to live.

—

A Pinterest board said, "Adventure will hurt you, but a life of monotony will kill you."

That's not like the smartest quote I've ever seen, so I'm changing it to this:

"Pursuing God will hurt you, but life without Him will kill you."

(Yeah, that's right. I'm making up my own quotes now. Gonna run my own Pinterest board, go viral and stuff...)

This road we're all on – this "life" – is full of pitfalls, and struggles, and hurts. No one ever said it would be easy.

Having God by our side gives us a "buddy" on the journey – a best friend whispering in our ear that everything will be ok, as we'll be serving His Kingdom.

But no one ever said you'll be comfortable, or living in luxury, or free from pain. Maybe quite the opposite.

There are thousands of examples of martyrs and people "uncomfortable" while pursuing God. I like to think of Paul, chillin' in prison, just writing away and jotting those letters.

Where would we be without his sacrifice? An entire chunk of the New Testament would be missing.

And I'm sure he didn't willingly choose prison.

But he had an attitude of, "I'm serving God, and it'll be ok."

So stop being a baby, and suck it up.

It'll be ok.

Part 2 - Life

COACH WATCHING

Every athlete is familiar with the phrase "Coach Watching."

It's when the coach is watching you, you act like a superstar. But when the coach turns his back, you suddenly slack off.

Sometimes you just want to coast through life without putting in any effort.

—

I played soccer in high school.

Growing up soccer was fun. There were rec leagues and pizza parties. You basically hung out with your friends and kicked a ball around. Sometimes the ball would find the net and you'd cheer.

But as soon as you enter high school, soccer turns into a nightmare.

Soccer is hard. Practicing every day after school is hard. Training in the scorching August heat in double-training sessions is the definition of hard.

Suddenly soccer wasn't fun anymore.

—

My biggest problem was running.

High school soccer wasn't about learning skills. High school soccer is about being in shape.

For some reason, high school coaches believe whatever team is in the best shape will win the game.

Why this logic reigns – I don't know – other than no one knows how to really play this sport in America to begin with, so we may as well run.

And to this day, I get PTSD from two simple trigger-words: "Jonesy" and "Brazilian Circuit." (Shudder…)

—

A Jonesy is straight up running and sprinting.

It's 5 laps around the perimeter of a soccer field, adding more sprints every time.

1st Lap: Jog.

2nd Lap: Sprint to the first corner flag, jog the rest.

3rd Lap: Sprint to the second corner flag, jog the rest.

4th Lap: Sprint to the third corner flag, jog the rest.

5th Lap: Sprint around the entire field.

The fifth lap is impossible. Inevitably there's some track star on every team who can accomplish this feat, but everyone else is sucking wind – and most likely, you're walking the last lap.

The simple trick to surviving, however, is to watch the coach.

Inevitably, coaches get bored. Watching 14-year-old boys run circles isn't thrilling entertainment.

If the coach takes a phone call – you walk. If he's looking at his notepad – you walk. If he's engaged in a hilarious conversation with the winner – you walk.

But as soon as the coach's attention is on you, you don't want to be caught dead walking, so you run (or waddle).

—

A Brazilian Circuit, on the other hand, is a station-based exercise.

Each station is a cruel torture device like tossing medicine balls, pushups, sit-ups, leg lifts, dribbling or shooting drills. There's an entire buffet of cruel exercises to choose from. Then after a couple of minutes the coach blows a whistle and you trade stations. You do this forever until you die.

My first introduction to a Brazilian Circuit was on a special Saturday training session (ugh) with the Girls Varsity team.

Why anyone thought to mix the boys and girls teams in a training exercise was a good idea, I'll never know – except to prove the girls could keep up with the boys?

After 20 minutes, everyone knew that was dumb.

The girls were dropping like flies. They were puking, being carted off the field, and the coach was hiding them in his car. It was like a scene from a horrible war movie. Bodies were everywhere.

Thankfully though, I had the best partner in the world. She was a coach watching superstar.

—

As the coaches were resuscitating a nearly-dead girl, my partner grabbed my arm and said, "Stop, no one's watching."

I was in mid-pushup and my arms were killing me. It felt like fire ants gobbling up my chest. I was thankful for the reprieve.

I wasn't too prideful to call it quits either. With her on the lookout, I felt entirely at peace to lay prone on the grass.

I needed a break. I was about to die.

She whispered to me, "I can't do this anymore. I'm going to pass out."

Yeah, man. Me too. But I wasn't going to admit that. Gladly

though, it was my new mission to make sure my partner survived.

The coaches returned and blew the whistle once more. It was time to change stations.

We had to grab the medicine balls and do some dumb medicine ball exercise. I was so exhausted at this point, I couldn't even remember how the station worked.

The boys were supposed to use the 10-pound ball, while the girls used the 5-pound one. Instead, my partner swiftly handed me the lighter girl ball, while she picked up a soccer ball (practically weightless).

I marveled at her coach watching ways. I had been given a gift from God and partnered with a wizard. She didn't want to do these exercises any more than I did.

But she was already seasoned, prepared for her coach, and his insane exercise antics.

—

Looking around, everyone else was in similar pain.

The track-star-ninja guy was off on his own gladly firing off rounds of leg lifts – he had already destroyed his partner and she was nowhere to be found – but everyone else was moseying around, heads on a swivel, watching what the coaches were up too.

No one made eye contact with each other, as no one would admit how tired they were, but everyone was exhausted.

Eventually, it was time to call it quits. Finally, our coaches returned and let us finish.

It was supposed to be a 2-hour Brazilian Circuit, but we barely cracked the first hour.

The girls went home. They were dismissed to lick their wounds.

The guys hung out for a while and pretended to scrimmage. We couldn't possibly waste a perfectly good day of practice...

But all our bodies hurt and we wandered around the field like zombies. We hoped our coach would disappear to McDonald's and get a burger so we could finally sit down.

We just couldn't do it anymore. We were done.

PHILADELPHIA

I hate Philadelphia. I've visited multiple times and lived there for a month. It's not a nice place and I hate it.

There are positive aspects to the city: The tourism sites are outstanding. The many museums are incredible and historical artifacts bring a tear to my heart. There's a feeling of awe and pride to see the cracked Liberty Bell and Independence Hall. It brings a sense of honor as an American – exactly what our country stands for and what we're all fighting for.

However, Philly is also full of poverty and despair. A block outside the beautiful city-center is endless miles of the underprivileged. It's a story of race-wars and economic disparity.

If North Korea were an American city, it would be Philadelphia.

—

One of the problems is all the money escapes the city. There are beautiful buildings and skyscrapers in the city. It's a thriving metropolis. You'd think Philly is kicking butt and taking names. You wonder how anyone could be unemployed in this bustling town.

Unfortunately, these "privileged" jobs are staffed by people living in the suburbs.

Imagine you live in your swanky McMansion, surrounded by like-minded peers in a beautiful utopia. Then you take a train – like the *Hungry Games* – and pass by endless miles of housing projects, abandoned buildings, and the homeless. As you pass in the speeding train, you don't even have to look out the window if you don't want. You can snuggle up to a good book and just pretend none of it is real. None of it exists. It's not your problem.

Then the train arrives at the city-center – the Hunger Games District 1 – where all the wealthy people hang out, drink, socialize, and be merry. At the end of the day, you can board the train again and return to your comfortable abode – and do it all again the next day.

—

So, when I had a chance to attend a stateside mission trip to Philadelphia, I said no.

"Hey, Joe. You're coming with us to Philadelphia, right?"

Nope.

No one knew my history or hatred for that city. They didn't know I lived there. They didn't know I preferred if it burned to the ground.

"I'm not going," I said flatly and plainly.

I had made up my mind. There was no point in me going. I had already been there and knew nothing I did could change that city. That city was bound to burn, like Sodom and Gomorrah – and I wasn't about to watch it fall.

Then days and weeks passed. I couldn't stop thinking about my hatred for the city. It was always on my mind like an ember had ignited and caught fire in my soul.

God has a funny way of forcing our hand and making us do exactly what we don't want to do.

"Fine, I'm going," I finally admitted reluctantly. "Just don't make me work with the kids. I hate kids."

(I'm sure you can guess how that played out... I'm pretty sure

God is a prankster. He's like a teenage jokester who thinks every-thing he says is hysterical. He's a punk.)

—

Once in Philly, we helped a new church run a children's summer camp (oh, joy) – my exact opposite of a good time.

One of our most difficult tasks was to hand out fliers to the surrounding community and invite kids to the camp. As of that moment, nearly no one was attending. I think 5 kids had signed up – and they were from the surrounding suburbs, being driven in (?).

So with fliers in hand, we set out to the questionable neighbor-hoods of inner-city Philly. If there was ever a time I wanted to call it quits, phone home, and evacuate myself out of there, it was then.

Being a door-to-door salesman in an upscale neighborhood is scary at best. To walk around the decaying streets of Philadel-phia is another matter entirely.

There are pit bulls barking and scary people answering the door. This is not a place I advise wandering around by yourself at dark.

Yet, I felt the severity of this assignment. If we weren't inviting the community NOW, no one was ever going to do it. This was the exact perfect timing, for them to send their kids to a safe place, and allow them a refuge in the middle of the summer, when everyone's out of school anyway.

And it wasn't like we were shoving Jesus down their throats (but really, we were...), we were just playing games and eating snacks. Who doesn't like snacks?

I felt the weight of that moment. I knew if they weren't invited now, by us, they would never get touched again. This was the exact moment their kids needed to hear the message of Jesus' love.

—

Suddenly, I knew why I was on the trip. This was my "thing."

I don't like skits or acting, kids or babysitting. But the one thing I excelled at, was sales.

I know ratios and numbers, I know the odds of looking for that one "yes" in a sea of a million "no's."

I can go up to someone's door, say hi, and invite them to church. I had already done it a million times as a trained sales professional. This was no big deal, this was easy and fun.

I lit up with the excitement and energy of it all. I loved handing out the fliers and talking to the people.

And then once we ran out of fliers, we went back for more and handed out a second round. There were kids in the street and teenagers willing to bring their siblings. It was amazing to interact with those people and to be a beacon of hope in their life.

And I wanted to keep going. I wanted to reach just one more person, to invite someone else, to reach the next house. Who knew where that "yes" would come from, and whose life it would change, but we needed to try.

—

The summer camp began on Monday with 10 kids. Strangely, and by an act of God, the week ended with over 70 kids attending. Where they came from, we'll never know, but it was an amazing sight to see God work.

And, as fate would have it, my heart slowly began to change.

There are amazing people at work in the city, set on helping the citizens of Philadelphia. Their love of the city was infectious – it radiated out of their soul.

We got to clean a park, repair the church, and play with kids. Every day was packed with excitement and adventure as I saw the city in a new way.

I walked away from that experience a changed man. Never in my life would I have known the love that existed in such a destitute place.

And as I left, suddenly I felt a longing to return, to help once more, the city I fell in love with.

Because, honestly, I love Philadelphia – it's a great place.

BUGS

Dead bugs are gross. And when it's a school project, it's even worse.

I had to make a "dissection box." I don't know what you call it, but I was in elementary school, and the assignment was to capture a bunch of insects and pin them to a board.

It was gross. I was terrified. I didn't want to touch any of the bugs.

At school, they gave us time to venture into the field and woods surrounding the building, to capture whatever insects were on the premises.

Then we'd poison them "humanely" in these death chambers.

Maybe I was 10 years old, I don't remember, but it was the hardest thing I ever did.

—

For one, I didn't like the idea of even touching the bugs. We had nets and would swoop them up, but then it was a circus trying to transfer them to Petri-dishes without it escaping.

Some of the more "manly" boys would use their bare hands. They were so cool. It was like they were teetering on the verge of insanity – because clearly, no one in their right mind touches bugs.

And two, I didn't like killing the bugs. It felt sad. To sit and watch while they squirmed in the poison, it felt psychotic, like we were playing God, and determining the fate of these helpless beings.

I didn't like it at all.

—

As some back-story, I had already been terrorized by crickets – hordes and hordes of crickets.

Our house was built in the middle of a gorgeous pasture, but in the center of that land was a colony of crickets who refused to move. We're talking millions of crickets here – like the epicenter of mating for all the crickets in the world – the "Garden of Eden" for crickets.

And of course, the crickets would seek sanctuary in our house.

We tried to exterminate them – nope. Tried to seal up the basement – nope again. Those crickets were nasty little vermin. They could somehow squeeze their bodies through the tiniest of cracks, shapeshifting their way into our home. It was a nightmare.

And killing them was disgusting. You'd whack them with a rolled magazine – but not too hard – or else their guts would explode everywhere. It was awful.

And one time I found a cricket in my shoe. Yep. By sticking my foot in there (Ugh!).

To this day I still bang out my sneakers every time I put them on. I don't trust anything.

—

So when the "bug-pin-board-project" came, I wanted to die. At the very least, I knew where to find a cricket…

With the project almost due, I was behind on my bug count – I needed more.

There had been slim-pickings on the school grounds. And whatever species lived there – like ladybugs – everyone else in the class had the same sample already.

Begrudgingly I had to borrow a net and capture more bugs at my house.

I ventured into the field, with net and Petri-dishes in hand, and became overwhelmed by the sheer volume of insects. Our field was swarming with life.

There were bees and crickets. All sorts of moths and fireflies. It was like a smorgasbord of bugs. I could pick whatever I wanted, and all within a 10-foot radius – I barely had to move. I was amazed.

With my net full and Petri-dishes packed, I stuffed all those beasts into the freezer. And there I found my answer to watching them die. I still didn't like the idea, but it felt kinder and gentler to think about them slowly falling asleep in the deep freeze. And this time I didn't need to watch.

(I'm sure my mom wasn't too excited about it though, finding a frozen bee next to the peas...)

—

I found myself in the field again the next day and the next. All of a sudden, I realized the bounty of bugs I had on my stoop.

I still had a fear of the bugs – because bugs are gross, obviously – but so didn't everyone else in my class.

I realized no one else had access to the enormous volume of insects like me. I was determined to go out there and capture the best collection of bugs I could find.

And I did. I had a really great collection.

Afterward, I kept that shoebox of bugs tucked in my closet. For years later (ick!) I'd take it out from time to time and marvel at my effort.

I had overcome an enormous fear of mine – and not only con-quered it but pushed past what I thought possible.

And to be honest, I had fun. It was a thrill to be out in that field, catching bugs, and doing hard things that no one else could.

I felt alive. And wanted to do it again.

SPIRIT AIRLINES

Spirit Airlines sucks. If you haven't had the misfortune of flying this horrible air-service – then save yourself the trouble and don't.

However, if you want a memorable story to share with your family and friends – then be my guest, and jump right aboard.

—

I heard horror stories of how bad Spirit was, but I didn't believe any of the hype. I figured these people were travel rookies, unfamiliar with TSA Security rules, and lacked common-sense travel habits.

I was like, "How bad could it possibly be?"

Because when my wife and I needed a flight to Puerto Rico for a business trip, the Spirit price was half the nearest competitor.

How could I resist? That was a deal too good to be true.

Alas – I was about to learn the error of my ways – and pay dearly for it.

—

The first mistake came because of my own carelessness.

We lived in Manchester, NH, and there's an amazing airport in MHT. People in Massachusetts routinely fly out of MHT, just to avoid the headache that is Logan Boston Airport.

If you have to fly out of Boston, then fine. But when you have a killer airport 10 minutes down the road, there's no reason to drive anywhere else.

So that was mistake number 1 – choose the airport close to home – even if you have to pay an extra $50, who cares. All that money saved is a waste if you have to spend an extra day just commuting to the airport.

And then tip number 2 is to always fly direct. Always. Especially in the middle of January, when snowstorms routinely shut down airports.

You're practically guaranteed to ruin your travel plans with a connection, or lost baggage, simply because you saved $100.

When you're stuck overnight in the Chicago airport, sleeping on a cot, you'd gladly pay any amount of money to be rid of your travel nightmare – but that's another trip entirely, and I'm getting off topic.

Spirit sucks.

—

Off to Puerto Rico, the night before, a blizzard rolled in.

We had an early morning flight out of Boston and had a decision to make.

We could wake up early, as planned, and fight rush hour traffic in a blizzard. But we'd be risking missing our flight, because of traffic and snow. Or we'd get to the airport fine, and only to find our flight had been canceled – then we'd need to drive back home and do it all over again.

As a travel pro myself – that option seemed ripe with mistakes, stress, and travel headaches. I didn't want to do that.

So instead, we drove down the night before and got a room at the airport hotel. All the stress would be gone, there'd be no driving in a blizzard, we could sleep in longer, and if inevitably our flight got canceled, we'd already be in a hotel and could wait an extra day – all the while enjoying a beautiful snow day in the city – it sounded magical.

Plus, as an added annoying bonus, I still had to pay for parking at Logan Airport – whereas Manchester I didn't – I'd get a ride or taxi or whatever. Staying at the hotel allowed us to park for free (yeah!) and get a chauffeured shuttle directly to our gate. Excellent plan, if you ask me.

However, the initial cost savings of the Spirit flight was now out the window, thanks to the hotel cost. So whatever, that wasn't Spirit's fault, as weather isn't predictable – but still, it was my fault for booking the further airport. I'm a moron.

—

The morning of our flight we woke energized and refreshed. Except for the scene outside looked like a Thomas Kinkade holiday card as a blizzard pounding the city. A Hurricane Katrina type blizzard. It was nuts.

We checked the flight status and every flight was canceled, except for Spirit.

"How?" I asked. As I spoke into the howling wind, no one answered my question.

How the heck was every other airline – Delta, American, JetBlue – all lit up in CANCELLED red letters – and one lonely Spirit flight status of "ON TIME"?

I shook my head in disbelief. "There's no way we're getting off the ground," I said.

I wanted to stay in the warm hotel, enjoy a leisurely continental breakfast and coffee, relax in the hot tub. I didn't' want the hassle of arriving at the gate, only to find the flight had been canceled.

—

So, we arrived at the gate and were immediately introduced to the insanity of Spirit Airlines

We quickly discovered we had to pay for our checked luggage and carry-on bags.

"That'll be a $150," the Spirit clerk said.

"Excuse me?" I coughed.

I knew checked luggage would have a fee – all airlines had recently introduced this cruel measure, and I wasn't foreign to the concept – but you're charging me for my carry-on bag?

How was that possible? I felt like I was boarding a flight with the mafia, and they made up their own rules as they went along, nickel and diming me for whatever suited their fancy.

It made no sense.

I was already calculating in my mind the apparent lack of convenience and cost savings of this trip.

Buying the ticket online and saving $200 over the nearest competition suddenly didn't sound like a good deal. When you're ripping people off and stealing their money at the gate, it certainly sets their vacation off in the wrong mood.

And Spirit knows exactly what they're doing – because they suck.

—

With the weather howling outside like a crazed wolf, the attendants kept reiterating our flight was "on-time" and ready to fly.

I kept shaking my head at the insanity of it all like I was being herded against my will to a flight that would never leave.

And I was partially right.

The entire airport was a ghost town. There wasn't a single soul in line at TSA, and we breezed through. That would have been nice in any other circumstance, except when the security officer asked what we were doing and what flight we were on – because clearly, we had to be idiots to be at the airport.

"Spirit," I said.

"Oh, good luck," was the reply, as he chuckled.

That should have been an omen, and I should have left immediately.

—

As we got to the gate, we sat around with the other lost souls bound for this dreaded flight.

Outside in the storm, the runway crew did a stellar job of cleaning our plane and spraying deicer all over the wings – because frankly, there was no other work to do, and no other planes– our flight was the only one with a death wish.

"It's still on-time," they announced. "We're waiting for a break in the weather."

A break in the weather? In this winter-monsoon? Who's making the decisions around here? I didn't want to get on that flight. It felt like a crime was about to be committed.

Still, an hour later, somehow, miraculously, we boarded.

And I wished I hadn't.

—

Our assigned seats were in the back row, with me in the middle.

Again, there's an upcharge to pick your seat ahead of time, and I really didn't care. But after realizing how horrible the flight would be, I regretted every prior decision.

The back row on the plane didn't recline. You're forced to sit in the upright position for the entire 3-hour flight. What kind of maniac made that executive decision?

Next, the seat and the legroom is much smaller than any other airplane.

I'm 6'1", which is kind of tall, but when I say I couldn't fit in the seat – I literally could not fit. I had to sit in the worst awkward position, just to cram my knees against the seat in front of me.

And then I felt bad for that person too – because they couldn't recline their seat either – my knees were preventing that from happening, even if they wanted too.

And my wife, who is considerably shorter than me, couldn't fit either – just to paint an accurate picture. Her knees were crammed. Like the width between those seats is smaller than the width of your actual leg.

Maniacal.

She displayed her discomfort by ramming the seat in front of her over and over again – the poor lady in front of her must have thought a toddler was sitting behind her, wailing away on the tray-table.

Then, a lady in the row next to us complained.

She said, "I have back problems. I can't sit in a seat without a recliner."

"I'm sorry," the flight attendant said. "I don't assign seats."

How rude.

But I'm sure the stewardess hated her company's policies – I'm sure as a human she felt empathy for all us poor souls – crammed on the airplane like a herd of cattle.

That's how Spirit displaces all of their horrible decisions like it's someone else's job and someone else's problem.

What a wreck.

—

We mysteriously took off and I was never more afraid for my life.

I find airplanes annoying and inconvenient – but not scary. I don't think I'll fall out of the sky or anything.

But this time I did. The takeoff was rickety like we were strapped into child's wagon and chucked down a rocky hill.

"Good luck," I remember the security guard saying.

Yes, good luck indeed.

I heard about older American airplanes being sent to retire in third world countries and living an additional second life of questionable safety.

Somehow Spirit got their grubby paws on these questionable hand-me-downs and now I was strapped to one.

I held onto my wife, as we took flight in the storm. She looked possessed, like one of those photos they take of you on a roller coaster. She wasn't having fun. She needed to puke.

—

Once airborne, I finally felt safe.

The last 24-hours had been filled with stress, headaches, and spending extra money.

This trip had turned into a nightmare and I wasn't having any fun.

At least now, we were on our way, and things would get better.

"Can I have water?" I asked – for me, for my wife, for my sanity. I just needed a drink.

"That'll be $5," she said.

I'm usually cool, calm, and collected. I see these stories of people throwing fits on airplanes and I don't get it.

But now I was furious.

However, I couldn't afford to get in a confrontation and meet the Air Marshal. I didn't have time for that.

Even though I was beyond angry – just nothing surprised me anymore about this company.

They charged for everything. Sodas and snacks, and other perks like airport transfers, taxis, parking, whatever. I was just waiting for them to announce a 50/50 raffle. The cheapskates.

—

The landing then was even worse.

As we sputtered into Ft. Lauderdale, the plane felt ready to catch fire. It made the most ungodly sounds an airplane should never make.

My wife too lost her mind. She still has a hard time flying – like PTSD – from this one single incident.

We ended up missing our connecting flight too, because of that initial delay. So that's just an annoying travel headache that's easily avoided.

But I was thankful to be off that flight.

As we rebooked a new flight for later in the day, I told the travel agent, "I couldn't fit in the seat." Out of mockery, like how is this legal?

Thankfully, she upgraded us to the emergency exit row. I could at least fit there, but it felt like a normal seat on any other airplane.

I really hoped there wouldn't be an actual emergency, because if people needed to get off that plane in a hurry, it wouldn't be good.

We also had Spirit flights coming home – which I considered rebooking to a different carrier. I went ahead though, and picked my seat ahead of time and picked the emergency row once more.

I didn't care that it cost more money. I was done with Spirit at this point and they could take all my cash.

I just vowed to never fly them again – and vote with my pocket-book.

They may make a profit in the near term, but I for one will never use them again.

And I'm certain to make sure everyone else know how horrible they are too.

—

One thing I learned, in this horrible travel adventure, is that things can always be worse.

Any plane I'm on now, if I'm uncomfortable, I always remember that awful Spirit flight. And I remember how bad things can get, and you can be tortured and tempting death.

Or when I'm miserable at work, and don't want to be where I am, I remember that Spirit flight too, and it immediately puts me in a better mood.

"At least I'm not on a Spirit flight," I think.

And then I smile.

AWARDS

I threw away my wife's trophy.

She ran in a 5k and received one of those flimsy medals for her efforts.

I dangled it before her and asked, "Want to hang onto your participation trophy?"

"Nope," she said.

I chucked it.

—

Our lives get cluttered with confusing awards.

We did some essential spring cleaning, tossing old garbage and donating what we didn't need – things that took up space in our lives.

But the 5k award was particularly interesting.

Why was this plastic medal, supposedly an "award" she worked so hard for, then forgotten about for years, tossed carelessly in a drawer?

And still, why was the medal so meaningless, that it had absolutely no value? The value of that trophy was exactly zero.

It was taking up space. It was cluttering our lives. It had to go.

—

There's a running joke about "kids these days needing participation trophies."

Any sport they play, they're immediately gifted with an award for their efforts. Win, lose or draw, it doesn't matter – because obviously, in the game of life everyone wins.

I don't want to explain why this is horrible parenting. We're raising our kids to be entitled brats, who don't need to try and get an award for showing up.

This isn't how life works. No one gives you an award for doing your job.

Sure, I go to work every day, and put in effort – but in the end, all I get is a paycheck.

If you worked, you get money.

If you don't work, you get zero.

Seems painful enough.

—

This one time, in band, I won an award.

I played the trumpet and in 6th grade won the Most Improved award.

The strange thing about the Most Improved award, is it means you used to suck.

It's like my conductor was telling me, "Hey Joe, in 5th grade you were horrible, but I didn't want to tell you. But now you've put in the work and got better – but don't get me wrong – you're still not great, there are other kids better than you. But at least now you're adequate."

As a 6th grader, I was over the moon. It was very exciting to win the Most Improved award. I felt special and valued for the hard work I had put into learning the trumpet.

The next year, band was great. I had fun. I was like, "Look out ladies, here comes the most improved trumpeter. Let me toot my horn in various ways for you."

I felt like a rock star.

—

Then, to my surprise, as a 7th grader, I won the Most Valuable Player award (MVP!).

"I won?!?" I shouted in utter shock. This was unheard of. The MVP award always went to an 8th grader, one of the older kids.

It's like the Heisman Trophy going to a Freshman or Sophomore. How is an underclassman supposed to win the best player in college football? It makes no sense, but it happens.

So I accepted my award with praise and adoration.

The year after that went well for me too. Here I was, now an 8th grader, and the reigning recipient of the MVP award. Clearly, I was the best, and this was "my band."

I was the leader, in charge, and ready to win the award for the second time in a row.

They may as well just slap my name on it and give it to me now. There was no other competition. Who else could they give it to?

And then, to my horror, I didn't win.

What?!?!

—

They gave the MVP award to my friend, who is actually an amazing guy.

And honestly, we probably co-captained that band, for two years running. It was our band.

And I was happy for him, he had worked hard too and played

really well.

But I was confused. I was the best – it had already been determined – so why didn't I get the award again?

—

A year later, I tried out for the Youth Symphony Orchestra (or whatever it's called). It's where the best kids go to play.

In the "interview" recital, I was like, "Hey guys, I'm really good because I won the MVP award as a 7th grader."

They were like, "That's nice, but it'd be great if you could stop talking into your trumpet and play normally."

I never got a call-back. They thought I sucked. That hurt my feelings.

Then later, I took some private lessons to keep up my trumpet skills.

My teacher was like, "You're not very good. I like working with you because you have funny jokes, but the trumpet playing needs some improvement."

So I quit that too. He hurt my feelings.

—

It's easy to be a "big fish in a little pond." You can put in marginally more effort than anyone else and be the best.

But enter the real world, and you're facing a world of hurt.

You're going against stiff competition who are kicking butts and taking names.

These people are putting in the time, energy, and effort, and going after what they want.

And you know how much time you've put in if you've given it your all, and tried your best.

Because ultimately, no one cares what "awards" you've won. All they want is to see you play.

WHEN LIVES COLLIDE

I saw a kid get hit by a car.

I was backing out of my driveway and saw two kids bombing down the hill behind me on bikes. I waited for them to pass because they were flying.

They continued to cruise down the middle of the street and toward an intersection.

"They're not going to stop," I said to myself. They were careening right for a stop sign, without a logical sense of road-rules.

Inevitably and horribly, a pickup truck came through the intersection at the exact same time.

Everyone squealed their breaks, the bikes included, but it was too late – the kid got hit.

Luckily, he slammed into the driver-side door of the truck – and bounced off like a ragdoll.

My heart stopped. I had watched these kids travel the entire way down the hill, and like a slow-motion movie into the path of the truck.

The kid was lucky to not hit the front grill, or stuck under a wheel. His fate would have been worse.

As it was, everyone was visibly shaken – me included.

I ran out my car, dialing 911 in stride, and came to the kid's aid.

He was young – maybe 10-years-old – and crying like a maniac. His forearm was bleeding and scrapped with road-rash – but he was alive, so that's all that mattered.

The ambulance came shortly because this was inner-city Manchester, NH, and the fire department was a block away. We could hear the siren squeal immediately after I made the call.

The kid seemed fine, with no visible broken bones, but he had just splattered himself like a bug against a truck, so who knows what else he hurt.

The driver of the truck too lost his mind. He stammered around and yelled, "Oh my God, oh my God." He was useless and a complete mess. His truck was fine with just a tiny ding, but I'm sure that guy lived in therapy for a year, just to shake the feeling of hitting a kid.

I felt bad for him. I felt bad for everyone.

I was just thankful everyone was fine.

—

Another time, a random woman jumped in my car.

It was the same intersection where the kid nearly died.

I was coming home from work and parked on the street.

I was messing with my phone for a minute (probably turning off a Taylor Swift album), as the passenger door swung open and a woman plopped herself in the seat.

"Oh, hello," I said politely.

I wanted to tell her to scram, to get the hell out of my car, but I didn't. There was something wrong with her, like she was sick, on drugs, and not mentally present.

I thought she might rob me.

"Can you take me to Charley's?" She asked.

"Sure," I said relieved. "Where does Charley live?"

"Over that way."

Ok. Let's go.

So I turned the car back on and headed two blocks north.

She sat patiently waiting, quiet, and fidgeting like she had something to be nervous about. Perhaps she was afraid of me? I didn't know.

But if she was going to try something funny – pull a gun or a knife or whatever – I was ready to ram my car into a telephone pole, all kamikaze-like. She wasn't wearing a seat belt.

Eventually, she piped up with proper instructions and directed me where to turn. It wasn't anywhere sketchy. It was a normal dude's house, right on a major road.

She prepared to exit my car, and I was ready to be done with this questionable character.

"Are you done drinking that?" She asked. She looked at my half-finished bottle of orange Sunkist soda in my cup holder.

"I'm done with it," I said smiling. "You can have it." – But I wasn't done with it. I love Sunkist!

She collected it in her hands like she was dying of thirst, and hadn't drank anything in a week.

"Are you done with those too?" She asked, pointing at my pathetic collection of change.

"That's yours. Take it," I said, offering the paltry 87 cents.

"Ok, thanks," she said, and finally got out of my car.

As soon as the door slammed closed, I burned rubber and peeled out of there as fast as I could.

—

On the short drive home, I shook my head in disbelief. What had just happened?

Who jumps into a stranger's car like that and demands a ride? Was she on drugs?

The only thing I could figure was she had been walking to Charley's house already and flagged me down like a hitchhiker as I passed.

Then when I pulled to a stop in front of my house, she figured I had listened to her request.

But she must have been thinking, "Who is this dude who picks up random women in the street?"

She probably thought I was a creep.

—

Now that I'm years past these events, I'm far from the city too. I'm living in my townhouse, out in the suburbs. And it feels safe.

It's quiet and the neighbors are nice. No one bothers each other. No one is jumping into cars or blasting through stop signs or crashing into each other. No one is on drugs – no one's getting hurt.

But it all feels so sterile. Like there's no interaction. There's no life.

It's like I'm living in my "high castle," far away from the troubles of the world.

I'm just out there, avoiding it all, and pretending it'll all go away – like someone else will fix it.

Yet, I think about the streetwalker and Charley, and the bike kid and the driver. Who are they and what are their stories? Are they ok?

Why do I get to live in a safe bubble, away from it all, while the rest of the world lives in squalor, and keeps smashing into each other?

How are we supposed to react when the problems of the city inconveniently invade our lives?

And does anyone care?

DISNEY

Growing up, I liked Disney a lot. What kid doesn't?

It's full of fun and magic. It's an escape from your normal humdrum life to something unique and special.

I loved everything about Disney – except for one terrifying thing:

The Haunted Mansion. That ride freaked me out.

—

I hated the Haunted Mansion and avoided it like the plague.

We'd be walking around the Magic Kingdom, having a grand ol' time, stuffing our faces with chocolate covered rice crispy treats and Mickey shaped ice cream bars.

But as soon as we finished taking a nap in the Hall of Presidents, we'd walk through Liberty Square, and my knees would buckle. I refused to take a step further. Because there, tucked in a dark corner of the park was the worst ride ever conceived – The Haunted Mansion.

I hated Walt for creating that ride. Why did he feel the need to frighten children at his wonderful theme park? It made no sense.

And every year, my dad insisted we go inside.

"Come on, it's fun," he said. "There's nothing to be afraid of."

Nothing to be afraid of? Have you actually been on that ride? It's like literally full of things to be afraid of. That's the point of the entire ride.

There's nothing actually fun about any of it – if they wanted to entertain you – it would have been called the "Fun Mansion" or the "House of Silly Things."

But no, it's haunted and full of ghosts. So, I'm good. Thanks.

—

I'd feel like a loser though. Me, my mom, and little brother waited outside.

My dad and sister were the only souls brave enough to enter.

This happened every year. Year after year.

There must have been one point when he suckered me onto that horrible attraction, and then each year after, I wasn't about to be tricked.

That ride is freaky from the start. Even the queue line out front is spooky with all the ghastly gravestones and creepy music.

And then the worst part, is once you get inside, you have to wait in the room which "sinks" into the floor. The lights go dark, and then BAM! – A creepy Disney cast member screams in someone's face.

Just horrible.

—

Around my teenage years, I finally had the guts to ride it. And it still scared me. But I didn't want to be a baby about it.

I hate how you can't see what's coming, as half the time you're turned backward. And then things are always popping up too fast.

There's a cemetery scene where goblins shoot up really fast and it's frightening. I'd have nightmares about that place.

But to survive with my sanity intact, I'd look away, stare at the ceiling, or close my eyes. As long as I could get through that part, everything else would be ok.

And then I'd have a feeling of relief at the end. Like a weight lifted off my shoulders.

In order to enjoy the rest of the vacation, we first had to survive the torture that is the Haunted Mansion.

—

As an adult, I had the pleasure of working at the Magic Kingdom.

One of the training sessions was an in-depth behind the scenes tour – pointing out hidden Mickeys, optical illusions, and Walt's creative genius.

And hands down, the best feature of the tour, was riding the Haunted Mansion.

The guide explained the history of the ride, the Imagineering inspiration, and the story driving it all.

There's a ton of character development in the ride, and an entire backstory of the bride in the attic – it's a wild ride as she jumps to her death and enters the underworld.

I never knew any of that, how is anyone supposed to know? It just seems like a bunch of spooky crap jumping out at you and scaring young children for no reason.

—

But after that tour, I couldn't get enough of the ride.

I absolutely insist on riding the Haunted Mansion when I'm at Disney, as it's one of the only rides worth repeating.

All the other rides are crap – It's a Small World – come on, really? And the Teacups – give me a break. If I wanted to throw up on my vacation, I'd go down the road to Universal Studios.

But the Haunted Mansion is amazing. I've probably ridden it over 50 times now and counting. I like all the different segments, the scenes of the story, and I stick my head outside of the cart, anxious for the next turn.

And there's hidden Mickey's galore. It's fun to spot those suckers and point them out to your friends.

I even got the pleasure of working at a special ticket, after hours "Haunted Mansion Party." It was absolutely amazing.

I'm like giddy with excitement, just thinking about it.

And can't wait to go back.

THE SUPERHERO BOOK

I'm a famous author.

Or, at least I used to be.

In elementary school, I wrote a best-selling book called *The Superhero Book.*

It was amazing and shot me to stratospheric heights of local celebrity fame.

—

My friend and I co-authored the book.

One day, we were doodling imaginary superheroes on scrap paper. Cool characters like the "Snowman" and the "T.V. Man". And decided they were awesome enough to paste into a book.

So we cut them out, carefully, and glued them on heavy white paper. Then we duct-taped the spine together. It was a masterpiece of third-grade art.

And then, the book needed words.

So we wrote their biographies in baseball-card style, like favorite food and favorite catchphrase.

We came up with some pretty funny stuff. We thought we were little comedians and everyone loved it.

—

The teachers loved it too. They made us visit the younger grades for '"reading time."

My friend and I would stand in front of all these little kids – like an author signing at Barnes & Noble – watching in awe as we flipped the page and read each of the heroes' likes and dislikes.

And then, my favorite part came at the end.

As a grand finale, the final page featured "The End Man." His body consisted of big bubble THE END letters. Just absolutely ridiculous after a long line of funky heroes.

His catch-phrase: "The End."

And then we'd slam the book shut. Stand to a thunderous applause and take a bow.

Priceless.

—

As word of our fame spread through the school, we inevitably needed a sequel.

Superheroes 2 was born. Another round of incredible heroes with little food allergies. It was epic.

And then, for an encore, we doodled up *Superhero Moms*. And then a fourth book in *Superhero Babies*.

We were oozing with creative ideas.

I had never had more fun making something in school as I did those Superhero books.

—

But then I experienced burnout.

We were famous. Everyone knew who we were.

Joe Shaughnessy

We'd be in the cafeteria, eating ham sandwiches and minding our own business, when an adoring fan would tap our shoulder and ask for an autograph.

Ugh. The first time was amazing – we had never felt so loved and adored – but after a while it got old. All those annoying little pests harassing us.

—

And then an adoring fan needed me to edit his story. (Because I was a famous author, obviously.)

The story went something like this:

7:00 AM, I woke up. Then at 7:15 AM I had breakfast. It was Frosted Flakes and it was good. Then at 7:30 AM the bus came. That was fine. At 8:00 AM school started.

Um, yeah. You don't need to be a professional copywriter to know that's crap.

"Maybe you could quit it with the time-stamping," I said as helpful advice. "And maybe ramp up the stakes a little."

Maybe you could do it like this:

At 11:37 AM the superhero arrived. Then a minute later, he saved the world.

Blam! Wow! What a story. It's full drama and suspense – oozing with tension and unanswered questions – leaving the reader wanting more. What a great start to an epic novel.

He didn't like my idea. He thought I was a moron.

—

Now, 20 years later, I think, wow, it was fun to write those stories.

I'd get sucked into the craft of it, designing the heroes and making funny jokes out of their statistics.

I mean we cranked out four books – for fun.

Like literally, who writes four books for fun? Only crazy people, that's who.

Why did I ever quit?

I didn't like all the attention. I didn't like feeling I was wrong. I didn't like disagreeing with people.

And it felt like I wasn't taking school seriously. There's like homework to do and tests to study for.

I'd hear: "You can create comic book characters in your free-time – because right now it's serious school time."

You're too busy studying history, math, and science.

In third grade, how are you supposed to know that creating superheroes is a full-time job? It's literally something you can pursue.

But no one ever tells you that.

Besides, who has time to write pointless books that no one will ever read?

Not me.

BATTLES AND WARS

I played with Legos wrong.

I didn't like constructing the Lego sets – like a normal person would – instead, I'd let them fight.

My parents bought me tons of Legos and it was awesome. My favorites were the medieval knights and forest woodsmen.

Since they lived in the same "world," I'd put them in hand-to-hand combat against each other, and they would fight to the death

Oh, yeah! Bring it on!

—

If today, I sat on a psychiatrist's couch and he asked, "Tell me about your favorite childhood toy."

I'd say Legos (and also Ninja Turtles).

He'd then psycho-evaluate me and be like, "Well you should be an engineer. Legos are the building blocks for great architects, car designers, and house builders."

Nope. Mr. Psychiatrist. You're wrong.

Because I'd tell stories and my Legos would fight!

—

Building the castles and cars was moderately entertaining. It was like working on a puzzle, finding the right piece, and stick-

Escape the Cubicle

ing it together properly.

But really, Legos are more like a weekend IKEA project your wife insists you build for her with mismatched pieces and asinine vague instructions.

It feels like unpaid labor – it's work – and it's horrible.

Once I was done with the Lego masterpiece, however, I insisted it stayed together. I didn't like rebuilding anything or taking things apart.

And I definitely didn't like making my own creations from scratch. I hated that. I just felt like more work.

—

One time, I built this gigantic castle. It was a new masterpiece to add to my collection. I couldn't wait to start storming the gates and protecting it with arrows. It was going to be epic.

After a weekend of building the set, it was finally finished. Yeah. But then I had to move it to my room.

I had built it in the dining room because that's where all the puzzles got built – with plenty of space to spread things out.

As I lifted it and carefully made my way to the stairs – CRASH! – I fell and dropped it like a moron.

It split into a million pieces and I wanted to die. I didn't feel like building that piece of crap castle all over again. My life was ruined.

—

When I'd sit in my room, I had two distinct structures – the medieval castle and the forest hideout.

The knights would defend the castle. I liked the knights a lot because they had cool helmets, armor, swords, and crossbows. They even had mean looking horses with matching robes and

167

colors. I had a ghost figure too – he was creepy.

And then the woodsmen were like Robin Hood. They wore green clothes, had bows and arrows, and funny pointed hats like Peter Pan.

I'd get them set up on either side of the room. Then they'd fight. They'd invade each other's base and try and steal the Queen and stuff. They'd betray each other and switch sides. And they'd definitely chop off those yellow Lego heads. "To the gallows!"

I was creating backstories. I'd be like, "This guy is related to him, and that's his wife. But this guy stole his wife. So he wants to kill him." And go – start scene.

—

I'd call up my little brother too and make him move around some of the characters – because I only have like two hands and these were some epic battles.

I'd tell him what their motivation was and what they were guarding. He'd be really into it too, and would happily let his entire team die for the sake of the story.

But really, I didn't know how the story would end – we'd have to fight it out and see.

—

In my mind, I've never stopped the Lego war.

They're still fighting in my head, switching alliances, and slitting each other's throats. I can't stop telling the story.

They've taken different forms and evolved – these are characters fulfilling fantasies and heroic stories we'll never get to live.

Sometimes it's just fun to tell an unbelievable story and play a game, with a bunch of plastic characters.

Because frankly, as we age, we've all grown pathetic and no one's willing to stick their neck out anymore. No one takes any risks.

So this is the only epic story we'll ever get to experience – through the imaginary lives of little yellow men.

"Off with their heads!"

BROKEN ARM

I broke my arm once.

The strange thing was, it didn't hurt.

I was playing first base in a baseball game. It was the first game of the year, in the first inning, with one out – and let's pretend the score was 1-1 and the batter's count was 1-1 too, just to keep the "1" theme alive.

The batter bunted the ball and the catcher threw to first. As the ball came at me, it drifted into foul territory. I stretched out my arm to catch it and collided with the runner. Ouch.

I never caught the ball. It flew somewhere into right field.

I didn't know anything was wrong at first, other than I couldn't feel my arm. My glove felt heavy and I couldn't lift it.

As I looked down, something was definitely wrong. A bone stuck up like a bone shouldn't. And thankfully it never broke the skin, but my wrist looked like a scene from a horror movie.

So I walked off the field.

—

I was fine.

Everyone was freaking out. No one knew what to do.

But I was cool. I was like, "Can someone take me to the doctor?" I was calm like calling for pizza delivery.

I had broken my arm – I wasn't dead – but knew it needed to get fixed, and sitting around the baseball field wasn't going to solve anything.

So an ambulance came – which felt like total overkill – and drove me to a hospital.

They drugged me up, knocked me out, and fixed my arm.

The next thing I knew it was the next day and I was back at home.

That's when the pain began.

—

I was given pills. Some insane pain reliever that sent me to the moon and made me feel like an alien.

I felt sick. Like I had the flu. I sat on the couch for a week to recover. And felt horrible.

I couldn't eat either. Whether it was the pills or the pain, I didn't know, but food and I weren't friends.

I lost 10 pounds that month – and being a thin kid already – didn't have much weight to spare.

I was in agony. That first week sucked.

—

Going back to school was fine. Everyone wanted to be my friend and sign my cast.

The cast was epic. It began at my knuckles and when all the way to my shoulder – a full-length cast covering my entire arm.

My arm was stuck in the shape of an L, bent at the elbow. I had a sling and had to hold it across my chest.

That was annoying and hurt. The pain never fully left either. Some days were better, but I had gotten off those insane pain-killers and switched to Tylenol – something to take the edge off without feeling like I was swimming in Fruit Loops.

—

After a month, that cast went away.

I had to exchange it for a smaller cast to cover only my forearm.

I visited the arm doctor and he cut it off with one of those crazy buzz saws that won't cut your skin.

Once that cast was off, it smelled like a sweaty gym sock.

"Ok, move your arm," He instructed.

I couldn't. My elbow was locked.

I tried inching it out of position and it wouldn't budge.

As I tried to force it, a lightning bolt of pain shot through my bone.

"Owwww," I screamed.

I wasn't being a baby or dramatic.

It was the worst pain I ever felt in my life.

—

He put the new smaller cast on and I was out of there.

On the car ride home I tried wiggling my arm and to get it moving again, but it still felt like a forest fire.

I couldn't do it.

After two days, of trying again, and slowly creeping my arm forward, I finally had it. I could fully extend my elbow again, but it had been such a difficult and painful process to do so.

That was rough.

—

A month later, it was time once again to remove the final cast.

I was finally done and my arm was fully healed.

I visited the same buzzsaw maniac and he chopped the cast off again. This time it smelled like dead fish.

"Ok, move your arm," he said again.

I looked at my wrist, which hadn't moved in two months, and knew what to expect. It was going to feel exactly how my elbow had felt before, having been frozen in place for so long.

And I was right.

I twitched it and it felt like the worst blazes of hell burning in my arm.

"I'm good," I said. "I'll stretch it out later."

—

It took a week to get my hand back and feel like normal. It was awful.

I would gladly break any bone in my body all over again, that was no big deal.

But the recovery process was torture. I have never been in so much pain, for such an extended period of time – I wouldn't wish it on my worst enemy.

It forced me to quit baseball too. The following year, I couldn't catch the ball. My arm worked fine, but I was so scared of getting hurt again that I ducked every time the ball came. I dropped ball after ball. I probably looked like I had never played baseball in my life.

I didn't want to break my arm again – I didn't want two months of torture.

So I quit.

CHEATERS

Baseball players are cheaters.

During tryouts for my high school baseball team, I realized everyone succeeded by cheating.

And it made me furious.

—

The first day of tryouts was nothing but running.

I knew this ahead of time. There had been a team meeting in February, as the coach told us not to bring a glove. That the first day of spring training we'd run.

That terrified me. I hated running.

I had already played soccer in the fall, and all we did was run.

I can't even recognize what a soccer ball looks like any more – but running shoes, and sneakers – yeah, we're pals.

The problem was, in soccer, I was always last. I sucked at running and hated it a lot.

—

One of our favorite soccer exercises was to go on a "tour." A tour meant a "tour of the city."

We'd lace up our running shoes and hit the pavement. And we'd run. We'd run until we died, then we hobbled back to the field.

Literally every time I was last. I couldn't figure it out, or how to be better. Everyone was just better runners than me.

And once, I pulled my calf muscle.

It felt like someone took an ax to my leg and chopped it off. I couldn't move it anymore.

I stopped running and fell away from the pack.

The assistant coach stopped with me, encouraged me, and begged me to keep running.

It wasn't going to happen. I couldn't move.

I had to walk 2 miles back to the field – and then my leg bruised into this huge purple spot to prove I wasn't lying.

That hurt a lot.

—

So when baseball came around, I was determined to not be last.

I trained all winter. I went outside in the freezing weather and ran around in the snow.

I did laps around our house, up and down the driveway, and sprinting up hills.

It was a lot of hard work, and I put in the effort.

I was so determined not to be last any more – and I knew the obvious secret – to train, to practice, to just run.

—

There's an old soccer mantra: "You can be in shape – or you can be in soccer-shape."

Soccer-shape is like hardcore-marathon-running type shape. It means you can run forever and never lose your stride. It means running for days, with a smile on your face, and able to have a full conversation with a friend.

Anyone who's played soccer competitively knows what I'm talking about – it's being in shape on a psychotic level.

At the end of the fall, however, I had lost my soccer-shape body – even though I still wasn't a great runner, it still made me stronger.

Sitting around all winter I had become sad and flabby.

Hitting the snowy slopes and running again was hard. I could feel it in my lungs and legs.

I had to try again, to get back into shape, before baseball tryouts began.

I didn't want to be last ever again.

—

Well, if you've ever watched professional baseball, I don't need to tell you that "being in baseball-shape" is not the same as "soccer-shape."

Baseball is full of large men who can't run, but will gladly smack home run after home run – think of "Big Papi" David Ortiz, or even Babe Ruth – there's just some big dudes.

So, at the beginning of March, when baseball tryouts started, I stood happily outside in my running shoes, looking at my competition.

They weren't in shape. I was going to leave them in the dust.

—

We took off running around the city on our 3-mile tour.

I was near the front of the pack in the beginning – as this is a good technique for staying in front – and inevitably the group thinned out as the miles past.

Somewhere around mile 2, the coach drove up and cheered me on.

"You're doing great, kid. Keep it up," he shouted to me out the window of his heated car. He was sucking on a donut and enjoying a hot coffee.

I gave him a thumbs up. I felt good, in shape, and like a rock star.

I had put in the hard work during the winter – when no one else was – and was already impressing the coach on day one.

—

It took me about 30 minutes to finish and I felt great.

I still had energy at the end and was able to finish at a light jog – not the walking that soccer had forced me to do and kicked my butt.

Rounding into the high school parking lot was the finish line.

There were 20 boys ahead of me – all upperclassmen, and in-shape dudes.

I felt great. I was right in the middle of the pack, and here I was, a lowly freshman.

I got some high-fives from the guys as I finished. I felt amazing. I was well on my way to making the team and impressing the coach – I had finally figured out how to run.

—

Then, to my horror, the rest of the team stumbled in right behind me. Like immediately behind me.

Like the remaining 20 guys, all big and out of shape, had been right on my tail.

"What the heck?" I said. Where did they come from? I had smoked those guys. They were eating my dust after the first mile. It should have taken them another 30 minutes to finish, at least – if not an hour.

I imagined we'd be waiting around the parking lot, playing

cards and bonding over hot cocoa and having a merry time.

But no. Everyone was back. Everyone was done. And it only took the last guy 35 minutes to finish.

I couldn't believe my eyes.

—

"They cheated," my new friend said to me. "They cut through a different block around the school. They probably only ran a mile, tops."

I was beyond furious. My face burned red, as I wanted to scream, but couldn't.

They had made me look bad. It made me look like I was close to the end – with the last place finishers – but I wasn't.

I was at the front.

No one said anything. No one made a fuss.

There was whispering among the better runners, but what are you going to do? Cause a scene, start a fight? This was supposed to be a team after all, and we support each other.

I don't even know if the coach knew. He had driven in his car, so he wasn't about to be out there running. It's not like he knew how long it took to run 3 miles around the city – he could barely walk himself.

Anyway, I felt good for my effort, and that's all that really mattered.

The next day, however, was something entirely different.

—

In the winter, all the fields are covered in snow, so we're forced to play in a parking lot. It's dumb. That's not baseball.

So, to warm up, the coach made us run 4 laps around a tiny city block – it would have totaled a mile – not too far.

But the better runners took off in a sprint, while the laggards struggled behind.

Again, I was up with the better runners, making good time.

And then we started lapping people. It was hysterical. These jerks were so slow and so out of shape. They couldn't even run a mile. If this was soccer, they would have been cut, for sure. What a joke.

So I felt great again, now that I was doing well, especially at something I'm not good at.

And I was excited, knowing the slow morons who cheated yesterday would pay for their sins today.

The coach stood and watched from the parking lot. He could see us run the entire way.

I finished lap 3 and had just started my final lap 4, but I realized most people had stopped. I was in 10th place, but only two other guys were behind me. Where was everyone else? Why were they already standing around at the finish line?

"Are you kidding me!?!" I screamed. How in the world was this happening? Again? I couldn't believe it. This was the stupidest group of guys I had ever met.

I was with the better athletes, running hard, sucking the freezing cold wind in my chest. This wasn't fun for anyone. No one wanted to be out there.

So why were they all stopping? Why were they cheating?

Unbelievable.

—

I finally finished that lap, pissed off beyond belief. It made it look like me and a few other guys had finished last.

As we came across the finish line, my friend laid into the rest of the team and let them have it.

"Hey, you stupid morons. We lapped all of you. You only ran 3 laps."

And they were like, "What, no we didn't."

It turned into a big yelling match. But this had been pent up anger from the cheating the day before.

The coach didn't know what to do. He was just like, "Well whatever, whoever needs to finish the last lap go do it."

A few boys owned up to the mistake – and went out and ran some more – but most didn't.

—

I was furious. It wasn't like they were cheating the coach or getting away with something – they were cheating me.

I had worked hard. I had put in the effort. And now they were making me look bad. They were making me look average – worse than average – last.

But I wasn't last anymore. No longer.

How was the coach supposed to know that I was a superstar? And had worked hard? And was determined to make the team?

I desperately wanted him to know who I was. I wanted him to be like, "Who's that freshman who's keeping up with the varsity team? What's his name?"

I wanted him to know me. I wanted him to know how much I cared – how much work I had put in – and how much I wanted to make the team.

But he would never know.

Because I got cut.

QUITTING

I looked like an idiot.

During baseball tryouts, I made myself stand out in the worst possible way.

During a simple running drill, I messed up.

The coach had us spread out and line up at each base. People at home would run to second, and people on first would run to third and so on.

It was a dumb, so whatever.

I had been standing on third base, but when the instructions came, all I heard was, "Third base will run to first."

Ok, I was set, and ready to show the coach how fast I was.

I was going to shove it down all these cheaters throats and show them I meant business.

So when he said, "Go," I took off like a rocket.

Except, I had literally run from third to first, in a straight line, directly over the pitcher's mound.

"Hey, moron. Are you stupid?" The coach yelled.

Everyone busted up laughing in an outrageous roar. The drill had to stop because of my stupidity. No one could believe the antics I had just pulled.

But I had no idea what they were talking about. Did I win? Was I like too fast?

Joe Shaughnessy

Another kid had to spell it out for me, while everyone roared in laughter.

I felt like the biggest dope on the planet.

—

Half the team had been cheating at running already and made me look bad for 2 days straight.

But then finally, I was ready to remedy the problem, because of the sprinting drill.

I've talked about how bad I am at running long distance – I just suck – so I was impressed that I was doing well at running in baseball, but only because everyone else was so much worse.

But sprinting, on the other hand, I'm wicked fast. Even in soccer, I was always the fastest one, or a half-step behind. I'm quick.

So when the time came to prove how fast I was in baseball try-outs, I wasn't going to lose.

But it didn't work out that way.

—

It was just one thing after another with that tryout. I couldn't get anything right.

And all the teasing made it worse.

Somehow, people at school found out too and had a good laugh at my expense.

I felt so dumb.

And it wasn't that I had just made a mistake, but that my running abilities were being questioned. Here was the one area where I really shined – especially sprinting – but the coach would never know.

It would have been fun just to make the team, then only be used to steal bases.

But now the coach would never know how gifted I really was.

It was like a racehorse had fallen in his lap, but all he could say was, "What's wrong with that horse? He's like a few straws short of a hay-bale."

—

That baseball tryout was like applying for a job with the mob – you needed to shank your closest competition when he wasn't looking and toss him under a bus.

Everyone was cheating and making me look bad – worse, it made me look like I was a loser.

I was furious. I had put in the work, but it wasn't paying off.

It was backfiring.

To make matters worse, I kept getting "shanked from behind like a prison riot," that it made me upset.

You know when you lose your mind over something outrageous, like getting cut off in traffic, that you end up making more mistakes after that. You can't think straight.

It's like you trip, and immediately get up and fall some more – instead of regaining your composure, breathing, and trying again.

Well, that's how baseball tryouts were for me.

Everyone was making me miserable and I was determined to try harder and to prove my worth.

But I ended up making more mistakes.

—

After that, I was a mess. I couldn't think straight. I was so mad at everyone.

On top of it all, I had broken my arm the year before in a baseball accident. Now here I was, trying to prove my worth, and that I was actually a competent baseball player.

But all I managed to do was screw up.

I dropped ball after ball. Any pop-up hit to me would fall and bounce against the pavement – nearly smacking me in the face.

It just ended up being one comical mess after another.

I wanted to quit.

—

I'm pretty sure I was a ball of tears as I begged my dad to let me quit.

"I hate it. I don't like it. I don't want to go back." I said, which was a pathetic plea.

How was I supposed to articulate that people were cheating, and I looked bad, and I couldn't catch the ball?

And most of all, I didn't want to play with those guys. It wasn't a team I felt comfortable with.

"We don't quit," my dad said. And that was the end of that.

I think he gave me a long speech about how we don't quit things and we need to finish what we start. Which is a valid life lesson.

I still think about that today – about what a new project will mean or a commitment before I join. I think about how much work something will take, and how much effort I'm willing to commit – and the time.

If I literally can't quit – then I'm thinking long and hard about the things I say yes to, because once I agree, I'm committed – I'm not going back on my word unless I'm forced out.

So, sadly, I was forced back to that miserable tryout.

But I had given up. I wasn't having it anymore.

I'm sure I walked a couple of laps when it came time to run – what was the point anymore? And I sat out a couple of drills. These people sucked and they were horrible at life.

—

When the final team announcement came – I didn't make it. My name wasn't on the list. Obviously.

But I was relieved. I had never been more excited to get cut in my life.

I don't know what I would have done if I made that team.

As I left the field, happy to head home, one of my new friends caught up to me.

"Hey, did you make the team?" He asked.

I shook my head no.

"It'll be fine," said. "You did really well in the beginning. You'll be ok."

He had been with me, running hard, while everyone was quitting and cheating.

And that's all I wanted to hear – that I had done well, and overcome my fear of running.

Because frankly, that should have been the only reason I got cut from the team.

I'm great at baseball.

But I can't run.

CAMPING

I hate camping.

I don't like the bugs, the cold, the rain, and especially sleeping on the ground – give me a nice, warm hotel room any day of the week.

But what freaks me out most about camping, are the ghost stories.

—

My dad used to gather all the little children around the campfire, then begin to tell the Tale of Three Fingered Willy.

Three Fingered Willy was a man, named Willy, who had three fingers on his left hand. My dad would display this in claw-like fashion as Willy went about his creeping ways.

Willy lost his ring and pinky fingers in a boating accident, or in a machine shop accident, or from getting chopped by a hatchet from some pesky kids.

However Willy lost his fingers, it always changed. It was like Willy was on a Choose Your Own Adventure story, but the one thing Willy desperately wanted, was REVENGE!!!

Ahhhh! Then dad would attack us with the three-finger claw again. Willy walked with a hunch too, like the Hunchback of Notre Dame.

He was a creepy dude.

—

Willy lived in the woods. He was a hermit.

And whatever campsite we were at, that happened to be the same exact woods where Willy was last seen.

Ahhhhh! What are the chances? We need to get out of here.

So dad would finish the story and properly freak us out.

Then, "Goodnight everyone, but beware of Three Fingered Willy. Buwahahahaa!!!"

And dad would leave to his own tent.

Us little kids would huddle around inside the little kid tent and stay wide awake all night long.

Any time we'd hear a twig snap, "Ah! What was that?"

We'd all go quiet and listen for more sounds. Then silence.

One time too, from outside, someone ran their hand across the latex wall. Oh. My. God. I'm never going camping again in my entire life.

The next morning we asked him. Dad promised it wasn't him. I sincerely do hope it was him. Otherwise, there's some pedophile wandering around campsites in New Hampshire – Or, it's Three Fingered Willy!!!

—

The strange part was, we'd beg for these stories.

"Please, dad. Tell us about Three Fingered Willy."

"No, I'm tired. Go to bed," he'd say.

"But pleeeeeeeease."

Fine. So he'd sit down, tired after cooking dinner, assembling the tent, blowing up the mattress, and all the extra work that goes into camping.

And he'd launch right into the story, with renewed vigor, and play the role of Three Fingered Willy.

Sometimes the claw hand would pop out of his chest too – like that scene in Alien – and devour a little kid. Gross.

But then we'd cheer with excitement.

It didn't feel like a proper camping trip until the tale had been told.

—

Granted, the tale of Three Fingered Willy became the best kind of babysitter.

We didn't dare leave our tent at night – refusing to use the restroom, risking our exploding bladders – and we never dared wander too far in the woods either, because, "What was that behind the raspberry bush? It just moved. Ahhhh!" And run back to safety.

If we had Santa to be afraid on in the winter – he knows if you've been bad or good, so be good for goodness sake – then Willy was our mystical guardian in the summer.

We were always on our best behavior and on diligent lookout for Willy.

Because, quite frankly, we didn't want to die.

SPECIAL OLYMPICS

One of the best days of my life was volunteering for the Special Olympics.

In college, a day was set aside specifically for volunteer opportunities. You could choose whatever project you wanted, but many students were encouraged to help at the Special Olympics, which was held on campus.

My first volunteer year, I didn't want to help the Special Olympics. It felt too hard, and not my thing. I think I fixed a computer or painted a fence – nothing earth-shattering.

—

But the following year I had a change of heart. I decided to help and do the hard thing.

The Special Olympics needed "buddies." You got partnered with an Olympian, hung out with them between events, and were a source of moral support when they competed.

That year I met Robert. And Robert was awesome. He was the best.

He won all the competitions, came in first place every time, and absolutely destroyed his competition.

It was great – and I felt extra special to be paired with him because it felt like I was winning too.

Winning is awesome, after all, and the only thing that matters.

—

Trouble arose, however, in the final event.

Robert was running down the 100-meter sprint when he fell. Face first into the track. Splat.

I felt horrible. I didn't know what to do. I desperately wanted to run to Robert's aid, scrap him off the track, and give him a hug and tell him it'd be ok.

I didn't need to do any of that. Robert took care of himself, dusted himself off, and finished the race with grace.

But he didn't win. He had lost. And all he earned for his effort was a scraped knee.

As he crossed the finish line and came to me, he cried. Big soggy tears soaked his face.

I tried to console him, and tell him it'd be ok. I thought his knee hurt him, but when he came to, all he could whimper about was losing.

He felt cheated. He wanted a redo. He wanted every other athlete to line up again so he could race once more.

Technically, nobody "won." They all got medals for their effort. Because there was no gold, silver, or bronze medal.

But to Robert, none of that mattered.

He just wanted to win.

—

I didn't know how to tell Robert that in the "greater-scheme of things" he wasn't that fast.

If I had been out on that track, I would have smoked them all – not to mention the real Olympics, with professional athletes, and record-breaking feats of human accomplishment.

Frankly, most everyone is faster than Robert.

But to Robert, this was the "real Olympics." This was his chance to shine.

I asked him if he wanted to race me, as a special consolation event.

He said, "No." I didn't count. I wasn't his competition.

At the end of the day, Robert's father picked him up. He asked, "How'd he do?"

I explained he had won every heat – but had tripped and fallen during the 100-meter – and was really upset.

"He looks forward to this all year," his dad said. "I don't blame him."

—

It made sense then, why Robert was so upset.

In the traditional world where he can't compete and is always seen as last or special, he's given one day a year when he can shine.

While he may not be fast in the real world, when Robert was pitted against others with similar abilities, he knew he could win.

When he could finally use his gift, and run past the competition, and finally be able to win – he couldn't.

He didn't want to run against me – he knew he couldn't beat me. He wanted to beat them.

I'd be upset too if I had to wait an entire year to race again, and finally prove my worth.

So that lesson hangs with me today – that there's always someone better than us.

But when we're in our little "bubble," we think we're special.

Because there's a little bit of Robert in all of us.

COFFEE

I ordered the worst coffee in the world.

I hadn't been to Dunkin Donuts in quite some time – I was taking a caffeine sabbatical, and we all know how long those last...

Anyway, I said to myself, "I'm going to get one of those frozen coffee frappes. Yum."

Starbucks has these and they're called "Frappuccinos."

I've ordered these from Dunkin Donuts before, but I mostly only get hot coffee and donuts. But I remembered their "Frappuccino" version is delicious and that's what I wanted.

I drove up to the window and placed my order.

"I'll have a large caramel Dunkaccino, please."

"A what?" Came the snarky voice through the speaker box.

I held my breath. I'm always two seconds from strangling the fast-food workers. I swear the only thing they're good at is getting my order wrong. I can't wait until the robots replace them.

"A Dunkaccino," I said calmly and with compassion. "With caramel. Large."

I paused. Silence.

"Do we have that?" She said, speaking to a manager. "Ok, yep. Dunkaccino. $2.03 at the window."

"Thank you."

Geez. It's like pulling teeth with these people.

I pulled around and waited far too long.

She finally popped her head out of the window and handed me my drink.

"Dunkaccino," she said. "Enjoy."

She gave me a large hot coffee. That's not what I ordered. The Dunkaccino is a blended ice drink.

"What's this?" I asked. "I wanted a Dunkaccino. It's a cold drink."

"No, it's hot," she said with a smirk. "And you're the first one to order it this year." Her smile told of something sinister at play.

What the heck? I ripped the drink out of her hand and sped off like a maniac.

I don't like arguing with people. If I disagree with how they treated me, I won't shop there anymore. I vote with my pocket-book – and soon you will go out of business.

This DD was in trouble. They were on my "out of business" hit list.

But what in the world had I ordered?

I sipped the drink and it tasted like warm sugary urine. Gross. Not what I had in mind.

I couldn't drink it.

I returned to work, furious, with my mystery drink in hand.

I plopped down at my desk and fired up the DD website. In the ancient bowels of their menu, I located the culprit.

A Dunkaccino, it explained, was a cappuccino. To make matters worse, it wasn't even a real cappuccino, it was the essence of a cappuccino, flavored with cappuccino flavoring.

Basically, it was the hot cocoa equivalent of a cappuccino and tasted even worse. It was literally a packet of imitation cappuccino dumped in hot water. Gross.

Not to mention it's a registered trademark. They've gone out of their way to protect this "intellectual" property. Why? I don't think they're in danger of anyone stealing this masterpiece.

I literally couldn't drink it. It was the worst drink I've ever had.

I dumped it.

Come to find out, DD calls their frappe drink a "Coffee Coolatta." Great.

Like that doesn't confuse a million customers daily. The equivalent drink at Starbucks is a "Frappuccino" but at DD it's a "Coolatta"?

Yikes. That's the worst marketing I've ever heard.

It's like if McDonald's invented hamburgers, and then Burger King goes and calls theirs a "hot hammy bun-which." But be careful if you order a hamburger at Burger King because they'll give you a ham sandwich.

What kind of illogical nonsense is that?

DD! Take that crap off your menu. You're better than that.

(But I'll still see you this afternoon for a "Coolatta." Because they're delicious.)

NINTENDO

I never got what I wanted.

I always wanted a Nintendo.

Every Christmas that was the primary item on Santa's Wish List – a NINTENDO in big bold letters. And circled, and highlighted. Every year he'd conveniently skip over this must-have item.

Sure, he'd remember to pack me Ninja Turtle action figures, and plenty of Legos.

But the Nintendo – nope.

And every year, I was disappointed.

—

My dad said it would rot my brain.

So I tried tricking him.

There were some educational video games for Nintendo. And some biblical ones too.

There was a game about Exodus. Moses would walk around and shoot Egyptians with manna. It was awesome.

But he didn't fall for my tricks.

Instead, he bought the family a computer.

—

That computer was awesome – and I'm sure like 10x the cost of a Nintendo.

So clearly, it wasn't the cost of the Nintendo that was holding us back – but the "brain rotting." That's always on the top of every parents hit-list. *Watch out for the brain rotting.*

I tinkered with that computer every day. It was fun to learn all the bizarre commands.

It came loaded with DOS – and if you don't know what DOS is, it's like typing commands into your computer. Imaging having to type into an iPhone to open Facebook. (Hey Siri, play Oregon Trail.)

This was the birth of the digital age, and I cut my teeth on this tech.

Then came Windows 3.1. And wow! That blew my mind.

(Which basically functioned *exactly* the same as the newer versions of Windows today.)

—

Then I got myself some computer games.

We had educational games like Where In The World is Carmen Sandiego. The box came packaged with an almanac – a thick book. You had to read through the book to find Carmen.

Then I went crazy and bought a normal game. I bought the very first version of Need For Speed – an incredible racing franchise which still exists today.

And when I loaded it onto our DOS machine for the first time – BEEP BOOP – the computer crashed.

What a piece of crap.

The computer tech had to fix it. Who knows how computers worked in those days. I think we needed more RAM to run the program.

But that guy kept my computer extra-long because he was playing the game.

He was like, "That game's cool."

Yes, it's very cool. Now give me my computer back.

—

But if you've ever used a computer (and I mean, who hasn't), you know they're a pain.

Even in the year 2018, there are still hang-ups and viruses. There are random crashes and unknown glitches.

Don't you dare call tech support either, because they don't know how anything works. All they'll make you do is restart the computer and hope for the best.

Geez. We're like slaves to these machines.

—

And before the year 2000, it was even worse.

They were always crashing and breaking. You had to be a geek to figure these things out.

I dropped my keyboard once – and BLAM – the motherboard died. Seriously?!?

But I was never getting a Nintendo, obviously, so my gaming addiction had to be resolved on the computer.

I'd rush home from school, ready to fire up Half-Life – and the piece of crap would be busted. The hard drive would be out of space, or it'd need a software upgrade, or the graphics card firmware became corrupted.

Crap. It was like Russian roulette with those computers – even worse than having to blow the dust out of those old Nintendo cartridges.

—

I was constantly AOL Searching (because "Googling" didn't exist...), perusing computer forums, searching for answers, trying solutions, and failing. Failing a lot.

It was trial and error, all day long, every day, every night.

This was the life of a computer gamer – and it strangely still is.

But I learned a lot about computers, about their inner-workings, and how to solve problems. It was like a passion of mine, to keep my computer running in tip-top shape, just for the sake of playing my favorite games.

Because when you're hankering for a killer round of Counter-Strike, and all you see if the blue screen of death, the first person you want to kill is yourself.

(I'm surprised the teen suicide rate wasn't higher back then – "Sadly, he killed himself because the computer didn't work. Bless his soul.")

—

Now, as an adult, I still never get what I want.

But I think God gives us what we need instead. Not what we want.

Like with the video games, if I had a Nintendo, I wouldn't have strived so hard with the computer problems – even if my brain would be fine, not mush. All those computer problems have toughened my resolve, and given me ways to solve issues without losing my mind (though sometimes I still want to).

For my current wants – seven years ago I wrote a novel. At the time, I thought it was brilliant. It should have been published by a Big 5 publishing agency and given a movie deal with Disney. And obviously, all the branding deals and action figures to follow.

But that book sucked.

It wasn't good enough. I needed to try harder, learn better skills, and try again.

So now I'm still trying to get published. I'm writing a thousand times better, and more clearly, but I'm still not published. It's irritating (at best) but I'm pushing forward, and trying harder, and not giving up.

If I had been successfully published all those years ago, what would that have taught me? What would I have learned?

It's like being famous when you're young – the Justin Bieber's and Selena Gomez's of the world – they haven't had time to develop, mature, or learn.

What if they had waited for God's timing, instead of rushing headfirst into something they thought they wanted?

Because once you get it, you can never send it back. It's yours forever and it's the only life you get to live.

So do you want a Nintendo now? Or would you rather wait, and be challenged, and grow?

And get what you need instead.

FIGHT

A man attacked me.

I probably deserved it. Because in the winter, I used to chuck snowballs at cars.

The boring cars would keep driving. Like seriously, how? We just lobed 30 snowballs at your car and you're going to keep driving and pretend like nothing happened?

The best cars were the ones who'd stop and get mad, yell at us, and honk their horn hysterically like notifying a listening adult – but all that meant was we won. We beat you and made you enter our world. Now you're ours!

Once, a dude in a sedan rolled down his window and started throwing things back at us.

WHOA! DUCK! We yelled and screamed and dove for cover behind the snowbank. "What was that?"

My friend got smacked, right in the head. PLOW! We thought his brain exploded and died.

But it was only snow.

That dude in the sedan literally took the time to pull over, pack some snowballs of his own, and turn around to launch a barrage of bullets back at us.

That guy was awesome – whoever he was.

—

We were always fighting and killing things.

My favorite game was Nerf War.

My younger brother would effectively be "king of the hill" and guard the top of the stairs. He had a gigantic Nerf Gatling gun which could fire off 20 bullets instantly.

And even though he was younger and smaller, he always had the advantage – that gun was ridiculously powerful.

But I wasn't entirely out-matched – I had a sniper rifle to take crack-shots at him – or when that ran out of ammo, I'd switch to the deadly powerful bow and arrow.

It was my job then, at the bottom of the stairs, to sneak to the top, or to shoot him in the process.

The rules of the game would often change mid-campaign. Like we'd start out by saying if you got shot it meant you died, and the other person won.

But inevitably, that wouldn't feel fair to whoever had lost, so the rule would change to three hits and you're dead – or the damaged body part would be lost.

Get hit in the right arm, and you lost function of that arm – that sort of thing.

And then if I still couldn't win, I'd call my friend to come over and we'd gang up against my brother. That at least evened the odds, because it was always so difficult to beat him.

My little brother was a beast at Nerf War, and it took all my creative energy to devise a way to kill him.

We'd try and flank him – sneak up the laundry chute on the

other side of the house – then surprise attack him from the side – totally unexpected.

Or one of us would draw his fire, and take hits for the team, while the other one ran up the stairs like a kamikaze attack.

It was the hardest game we ever played. But it was also the most fun, as each round lasted for hours.

I'm sure it drove my mom crazy too. She'd just shake her head at the insanity of the little boys creating total war on the staircase.

And of course there'd always be a temporary ceasefire when mom needed to go upstairs – inevitably I'd try and use it to my advantage and sneak up behind her – there was technically no way to cheat at Nerf War – because there are no rules in war.

At the end of the battle, no matter which side won or lost – but I normally lost – we'd evaluate the battlefield and laugh at the carnage in our wake. The sheer volume of bullets and shrapnel strewn about our house felt like the hardwood floor had been covered in a new Styrofoam carpet. You needed to shuffle your feet to walk without tripping and kick a wave of rubber bullets in your wake.

—

There's the topic of gender-specific toys – should you give a boy a truck, and a girl a doll.

Or is it safe to let boys play with fake weapons – like Nerf guns?

I don't know the answer to any of those questions. I had Nerf guns growing up. I turned out moderately well adjusted – I'm not some violent psychopath, except for the rare road-rage outburst – I don't even own a real gun as an adult.

But I know this: With or without those guns, I was going to find a way to kill something.

I've talked about my affinity for playing with Legos wrong and wanting them to engage in mortal combat.

And man, if there are woods around your house, those trees are guaranteed to become forts, and the branches growing off them into swords – and probably with intentionally sharpened ends, for killing stuff, obviously.

The forest in the back of my house was like a portal to a fantasy world. As soon as you stepped into the shadow of the woods, you were transported somewhere else.

Cops and robbers, dungeons and dragons, ninjas and karate killing time. Whatever. It was all awesome. The possibilities were endless in those woods.

And the stick swords we'd create were epic.

I found this long hairy branch, that inevitably had to be used as an elder wizard wand – it's like something you'd see out of Harry Potter.

I played with that thing forever, and found its lost cousins, and gathered them all up. It felt like lost treasure on our property.

Come to find out, that was poison sumac, or something similar, and burst my skin into an itchy tumor-ridden strawberry field. So that sucked.

My mom thinks I was allergic poison ivy – but I think it's because I was wearing that stupid branch all over my body and using it like nunchucks – because it was ninja time.

But I didn't care about the consequences – that branch was the best and needed to be owned.

—

Lately, we've been driving home, finding "guards" on patrol at our community gate.

There's a gang of heavily armed boys, fully stocked in Nerf gear, holding up the palm of their hand like a police officer and shouting "stop."

I'm sure their mom is annoyed with the rough-housing and war-antics and has kicked them out of the house – perfectly unaware they're now terrorizing the entire community.

"Don't stop," I tell my wife. "You'll just encourage them."

The best way to deter a little boy is to burst his fantasy bubble. Tell him it's not real and he'll go off and cry.

I thought how awesome it'd be to have weapons of our own, packed and ready in the car. Nerf weapons or water guns would be ideal.

Those boys would love it, to get a "drive-by" shooting with a passing car.

But we don't. We don't want to encourage them. It's already annoying that they're out there as much as they are.

Besides, it's a small community. I'm pretty sure they could find our car and enact revenge. I'd wake up to find our car egged, toilet papered, or a broken window, and that feels like too much effort to deal with.

So we don't.

Besides, I'm too old. And I'm done fighting.

I SAVED A BABY

I saved a baby from a burning building.

Ok, well, the building wasn't on fire, but it felt like it.

Regardless, there was still a baby that needed saving and I jumped into action.

—

Late at night, I was sitting at home watching reruns of Sailor Moon, when I heard a panicked knock on my door.

Obviously, I ignored it.

Only psychopaths knock on doors that way, and I didn't want to meet them.

Unfortunately, the knocking pounded again before I could even dip a tortilla chip for a second round of queso.

"I'm coming, I'm coming. Geez. Crazy psychopath. Give me a minute."

I like lounging around in my underwear, so I needed a minute to toss on running shorts, a plain t-shirt, and flip-flops.

I answered the door, and there staring me in the face was the image of the most frightened girl I had seen in my entire life.

You know when someone's about to cry – they have that puppy-dog look in their eyes – that's how she pleaded to me, for desperate help, without ever saying a word.

"I'm your neighbor," she explained, pointing to the door across the hall.

"Hi," I said, perplexed. I had never seen her before.

I didn't know if she needed to borrow sugar, or if she desperately needed to sell her last batch of girl scout cookies – because we all know what slave-drivers those women scoutmasters can be.

"My baby is locked inside my house," she said in tears.

"What?"

How is that even possible?

She continued, "I ran out to get groceries from my car, and left him inside. He must have managed to crawl up the door and grab the deadbolt."

"Don't you have the key?"

"There is no key. The deadbolt is only accessible from the inside. And my cellphone is in there. I wanted to borrow your phone to call my boyfriend at work."

Wow. What a bizarre set of circumstances.

"What's your boyfriend going to do about it?" I asked.

"I don't know what to do," she cried. "It's his name on the lease. I need help."

Ok.

"I'll help you," I said. "But your boyfriend can't do anything if there's no key."

What the heck? How do I get a baby out of a locked door on the second floor of an apartment building?

My mind raced into solution-mode. How could I launch myself into that room and free the kid?

"This is what we're going to do," I said. "We can either call the property maintenance man and see if he has access. Or we can call the cops, but they're going to break your door open."

"Can we do both?" She asked.

"Sure."

—

I ducked back inside to grab my lease paperwork. The maintenance number was there, but we were practically on speed dial at this point, because the building was assembled using toothpicks and rubber cement – that place sucked.

It was 10 PM, but I called him anyway because it was an emergency.

"What do you want?" He answered grumpily.

"My neighbor's baby is locked inside the apartment," I explained.

"Can't you unlock the door?"

"There's no key," I said. "It's the deadbolt. It's only accessible from the inside."

"Doo-doo," he had more creative language, but the essence is there. "That's right. Sorry dude," he continued. "If this is an emergency you need to call the police." He hung up.

Jerk.

"He can't help," I told the panicked girl. "I'm calling 911. You don't mind if they bust down your door?"

"What's that going to cost to repair?" She asked.

I shrugged my shoulders – but only because that's the answer I give to all questions.

$1. $10. $100. $1,000. Who knows? Do you want your baby back or not?

I called.

—

"911, what's your emergency?"

"There's a baby locked in a house and there's no key," I said again.

"Can't you pick the lock? If we send the fire department they're going to destroy the door."

I was sick of explaining the asinine circumstances at this point.

"Do it. Break it down."

She hung up on me. What was with these people?

I was about to give my phone to the girl, so she could at least give her boyfriend an update – but my phone turned into a useless brick.

911 took over the phone. It changed into "emergency mode" and was like a GPS tracking beacon.

"Hang onto this," I told the girl. "When this turns off, or the cops get here, you can call your boyfriend. But in the meantime, do you think any of your windows are unlocked?"

"They're not. They're all shut."

Geez, woman. Throw me a bone. You live on the second floor. It's not like anyone is going to crawl up there and rob you.

Except for me. Because that's exactly what I did next.

"I'm still going to check," I said. "If the cops get here, they're going to bust the door open like a scene from Die Hard."

I didn't know what to imagine. Cops with battering rams? Explosive devices? How do you open a door without a key? Kick it open? No.

I didn't have a ladder. But I'm friggin' 6 feet tall and built like a spider monkey.

I needed to climb to reach her balcony.

I kicked off my flip-flops – useless footwear – and brought the tallest thing I could find – the bar stool from my house. I scrambled up that thing, and then circus climbed up to her railing and pulled myself onto the balcony.

I could then look into her apartment. Her baby – a toddler – was leaning against the front door, waiting for his mom to return.

"Holy cow," I said.

I checked the slider – locked. And a window – double locked. Dang it. Should I bust a window open? What's the cost of a broken window vs. a broken door? Did it even matter at this point?

We heard sirens in the distance. They were close.

She was finally on the phone with her boyfriend. He said, "I'm at work. What do you want me to do about it? Call the police."

Nice.

—

I shouted down to her, "I can see your baby," I said. "He's alright. He's sucking his thumb. I'm going to stay up here though. If they break that door I can make sure he's far away from it."

That felt like a weird plan. I'd be hanging out on a balcony while the cops showed up. Suspicious at best. But I also didn't have a way back down. I'd probably break my neck.

The cops came, and the fire department too. I could hear the conversation as the lady explained.

"Can't you get a spare key?" They asked.

Geez. Everyone was collectively full of unhelpful solutions.

"Alright, we'll bust the door open. Get the Jaws of Life."

I didn't even know what the Jaws of Life were before that. I had heard about it but never seen it. It's a tool the fire department uses to pry open wrecked cars and wiggle people free.

I looks like a robot claw. Add some missiles to that sucker and it'd be a sweet Transformer hand.

As they got the claw ready, a cop shined his flashlight on me and into the bushes below, checking out my cool barstool.

I stood there, half-naked, shoeless, and a t-shirt. I looked like a trailer park redneck.

"What are you doing up there?" He asked.

"Trying to save the baby." Idiot. What a moron.

"Come down from there," he ordered me.

"How about you open the slider and let me in," I said back.

He wrinkled his mustache and considered my logic. Then he silently disappeared to finish a donut.

The fire department was awesome though and worked quickly.

I couldn't see from their vantage point – as I was obviously on the balcony – but I slowly saw the wall begin to bend and the door creek wide open.

The baby scattered too. As soon as they powered up the machine, it sounded like a chainsaw, the baby ran away and hid on the couch.

"He's ok," I yelled below. The girl demanded updates every ten seconds on her child's vital signs.

And the door finally burst open. It did look like an explosion – because the sidewall, that thing bent in a way a wall shouldn't.

Replacing a door seemed straightforward, but the maintenance man was going to have an aneurysm trying to fix that screwy wall.

That's what he gets for being a jerk.

—

The cops entered the apartment and made sure everything was fine. The girl pushed passed and swooped up her child.

Everything was great. It was going to be ok.

They mingled about, relieved about the safety of the child, and chatted among themselves – they had enough time to break out champagne and serve shrimp cocktail.

"Hey, I'm still out here. Let me in," I shouted and banged on the sliding glass window.

Like seriously, they were totally going to leave me out there.

Finally, I scampered through the destruction, and with bare feet, tiptoed VERY carefully like John McClane, hobbling over broken shards of glass – that's a Die Hard reference.

That's the thanks heroes get, a bunch of splinters and bloody feet.

I gingerly hobbled back downstairs, got my barstool back, and found my phone tossed in the grass.

Seriously?

Then I rudely pushed by all the emergency crew milling about by my door.

I sat back down, tired and exhausted, and resumed my anime episode which had been rudely interrupted.

An hour later my wife came home.

"Why does our neighbor have police tape across their wall? And where's their front door?"

"I did that," I said. "I had to save a baby."

EUROPE

I almost died.

I walked into the street in England – and WHAM! – a mini cooper buzzed by me, nearly knocking me on my butt.

Whoa.

I was literally a millimeter from death.

My friend yanked me back to the curb.

He was like, "Whoa, dude. Cars have the right-of-way in England."

Nice. That would have been excellent to know BEFORE I set foot on British soil.

Like holy crap, that should be a PSA announcement on the plane flying in:

"Where's this plane from, America, ok, let's tell them not to walk in the street."

Geez.

—

We got robbed outside the Notre Dame cathedral.

In the park surrounding the church, a guy was covered in pigeons. Literally covered in pigeons. I have an old MySpace video to prove it.

And it was hysterical. He tossed handfuls of breadcrumbs and stood with arms outstretched like a scarecrow. The birds went nuts. They climbed all over him. It was the funniest thing I had ever seen. I laughed very hard.

Then we were tapped on our shoulder by the sweetest little French girl I had ever seen.

"I lost my passport and don't have any money to fly home. Can you spare $20?"

My immediate answer, "No."

This was obviously a scam. Asking for help from Americans outside of a tourist attraction isn't exactly the first step I'd take in a similar situation.

Let's go.

My friend is nicer than me though, and he gave her the money.

"Can I have some more?" She asked. "I really need help and flights are expensive."

"No, we're leaving," I said. And we did.

As we walked away, the girl approached another tourist enamored with the pigeon-man's antics.

Were they working together? They had to be. What a brilliant way to single out tourists willing to help.

Make them happy, then stick 'em with a cry for help. Strange, but effective.

"If anyone bumps into you now, make sure you have your hand on your wallet," I said. We were obviously in the epicenter of thieves and had to be vigilant.

A bump-n-run mugging wasn't out of the question, especially since we had revealed where our wallets were hidden.

Thankfully, we escaped without incident.

—

While in Paris, I was tired of eating their crappy food and ordering mystery items off French menus.

I know right, poor entitled American, can't read the French, boo-hoo.

Shut up. You don't know nothing.

England's cool because it's still English, with a few foreign customs to make it interesting. Even Italy isn't so bad, people are nice enough to speak English.

But once you get to France, they're like, "Forget you, you're in France now. Speak our language or die."

I was sick of their snarky attitude so I went to a KFC, Kentucky Fried Chicken – to get a proper American meal.

But you guessed it, the entire menu was in French.

Come on! Geez.

Luckily, the menu included pictures, which looked remotely like chicken food.

"I'd like the number one meal," I ordered.

"Bienvenue french-blah-blah-blah," the cashier said.

"What? I don't speak French. I just want the number one meal. That one," I pointed to the menu.

She spoke deep and long French back to me like she was reading a novel.

"Listen, I have no idea what's going on here. All I want is some chicken. Here's some money. Just give me whatever. I don't care."

She spoke more. Asked more questions, and waited for my reply. With a stupid smirk on her face.

Was this a joke? I'm nearly certain everyone in France speaks passable English. They just refuse to do it. Bunch of jerks. Geez.

So I shrugged my shoulders and waited. I hoped she would just take my money and give me some food – because I KNOW she understood what I said and was being difficult about it.

She gave up on me, turned around, and collected a basket full of chicken tenders, fries, and a Coke.

"Thank you," I said, genuinely appreciative for the food. "And I know you understand what Thank You means too." And walked away.

"Merci beaucoup," she said to me.

Whatever. At least I didn't need to starve again or rely on another baguette.

—

Here are the Top 4 Tips for visiting France:

#1. Eiffel Tower is stupid and overrated. It's just the tallest building in the area. Not interesting.

#2. Notre Dame is dumb. It's a church.

#3. The Louvre is miserable. You'll spend 2 hours waiting for tickets. Then wait another 2 hours in a specific line for the Mona Lisa – which isn't anything special and looks like a fake poster (like they'd really let you see the real thing, come on...) Then wander around all day looking at the same art from back home. Dumb.

#4. The miniature statue of liberty in the Seine River is the coolest thing in Paris because come on, America, right? And there's no line. The French think it's dumb.

—

At a corporate dinner, I got in an argument with a waiter.

"Would you like some wine, sir?" He asked.

"Sure, what kind is it?" I asked.

"It's red, sir."

"Right, but what's the grape variety?"

"Red."

Really? It's red? Are you a moron? Is this your first day on the job? What kind of Mickey-Mouse-Operation is this? Where's your boss?

I figured he must be new – or a jerk – so I gave him the benefit of the doubt.

"Can I see the bottle?" I asked.

I grabbed it out of his hand and inspected the label for myself.

It was from Bordeaux-blah-blahdy-blah – I had no idea what it said. I flipped it over and it read more of the same. All in French. All indecipherable.

"Looks perfect," I said. "I love this kind."

I have no idea what it was. It tasted like Pinot Noir. And not much to write home about.

Why did everyone rave about French wine? It made no sense.

The following morning we had a wine tasting at 10 AM. I didn't want to drink wine that early in the morning, but when you're in France and are offered a wine tasting, you go.

Thankfully, the French host was nice. He explained why the French are snobs about their wine.

"Because," he explained, "the Americans have bastardized the wine industry and made it into a marketing machine."

USA! USA!

The French only have two varieties of wine – red and white – because literally, that's the only two types you can make – and rosé, and sparkling, but that's different.

So each vineyard makes their version of red and white wine, using whatever grape. And each vineyard, with favorites like

Bordeaux or Burgundy, has a unique flavor, thanks to soil and aging and whatever.

That's all I know. That's like the tip of my wine-iceberg.

But the Americans have taken the winemaking industry to a whole new level, mixing blends and focusing on different grape varieties. So you get things like Cabernet Sauvignon and Merlot, with nice artificial smoky flavors – a big huge marketing machine to crank out distinct and unique tastes – yum.

But my biggest takeaway, the wine guy said this:

"The French hate the American wine industry. They refuse to acknowledge the grape variety, only ever referring to the vineyard it came from, or red or white."

Ha! I knew it. That waiter was being a jerk.

Stupid French people. You're not fooling anyone.

MAGIC GENIE

I used to pray to God like a magical genie.

Like God was a funny Robin Williams type character, just waiting to pop out of a lamp and grant me three wishes on the streets of Agrabah.

Because in 3rd Grade, I needed his help: I didn't study for a math test.

I snuck out of class, right before the multiplication quiz, to use the restroom.

But what I was really doing was praying.

I stopped at the water fountain in the hall, pretended to drink, and made sure the coast was clear.

Then I dropped to my knees, clasped my hands, and prayed right in front of that fountain – like it was some sort of holy relic.

"Dear God," I prayed. "I know I didn't study, but I really need to pass this test. Please calm my nerves and give me the answers. Amen."

I shot straight to my feet before anyone was the wiser, and headed back to class with a skip in my step. With God on my side, I was ready to ace that quiz.

Obviously, I failed.

Any moron will tell you God doesn't work that way. He doesn't care about your success. If you didn't study, you'll fail. Plain and simple.

Yet, strangely, I felt at peace. I wasn't nervous.

—

Then I bought a lottery ticket.

As a young adult, I didn't have much going for me. I worked a miserable job in retail, without a clear direction for my life.

But one thing I knew for certain, was that God wanted me to win the lottery.

The Powerball had climbed to historic heights: $400 million dollars. Wow. Most of us can't even appreciate a number that large.

As the winner, you'd instantly be thrust into the upper 1% of the wealthy elite, able to buy whatever you desire, without a care in the world.

And you'd certainly be happy forever. Because, obviously, money equals happiness. Duh.

I also knew I had better motivations with my winnings. I'm like smarter than most people, understand taxes and interest rates, and would use the money for good.

So I bought a single ticket with God in mind.

"Dear God," I prayed. "I don't have a vision for my future or where my career is taking me, but I promise if I win the Powerball, I'll give you all the praise."

I thought, maybe 50% of the winnings should go to the church. Could you imagine that, a church with a single check for over $200 million dollars? Wow. I would be the most generous person in the history of the world.

And just imagine what good the church would do with all that money. They'd probably build more empty building that no one would use, and would rot away in another 50 years. What a great treat for the church to do more of God's work. Certainly,

God wants more buildings in his name – and I'm the one who's going to build them for Him.

And I made side deals with God too – like I wouldn't own too many houses, and maybe I'd buy a new car, but only one at a time – because obviously, a garage full of high-end exotic vehicles is self-indulgent.

But when the time came for the drawing, I had my ticket in hand and watched as the numbers flashed across the screen.

Nope. Nothing. Nada. I didn't even get one number right.

What the heck God? I thought I prayed to you and we discussed this? Were my proportions wrong? Did I need to give you more? Like is 90% better?

I did a quick calculation, and yep, I could still live on 10% of $400 million dollars – $40 million dollars would be rough, but I'd make due.

I just messed up. I had been too greedy. I would need to try again.

—

Now, as a productive adult, I find myself doing more of the same.

The prayers are different. I'm not praying for money or things I haven't worked for, but what's the difference? I'm still sugar-coating my prayers in selfish desires.

I'm like, "God, please take this pain away. I don't want to be miserable anymore."

But what am I praying for?

Am I praying for success? For a good job? For a pain-free life? For happiness?

Does God even care about any of that crap?

I'm pretty sure he thinks I'm a moron.

He's like, "Quit it with all that self-indulgent garbage and let me work, dude."

God is rude sometimes. He's snarky. But he has to be.

Because we're never listening. We're too busy talking to ourselves.

QUIET

I worked for a "large retail store" and avoided my boss like the plague.

I'd come in every morning, say "hi," and get grief in response.

She'd say, "Why is the store a mess? The reports haven't been cleared. There are damaged goods left undone."

There'd be no greeting in return. Just complaints – like a horrible guttural reaction.

It's 7 AM, for crying out loud. Can't I settle into work before the complaining begins?

It wasn't like these were real concerns either – just stuff at the top of her head, imaginary complaints. And not even my responsibility.

I always did good work. She'd complain about other people's issues and throw it on my plate.

Frankly, I'm not sure "hello" was in her vocabulary.

—

Eventually, I stopped saying hi.

I'd walk in, see her down the hall, and I'd run the other way. Like literally run.

If I talked to her for a half-second, it would ruin my day. She had nothing positive to say. Ever.

Some days, I'd manage an entire shift without ever seeing her. 8

full hours. It was an epic feat of boss-avoidance.

What made it fun, was she wore a giant carabiner around her belt with 30 keys. She jingled so loudly down the aisle it sounded like Santa was coming to town.

Sometimes I'd hear my name over the intercom, as they'd be looking for me. I always responded, and was proactive, giving an update or my position.

But if was face-to-face with her, I wouldn't utter a word or initiate a conversation. It'd be like poking a bear and she'd utter more useless nonsense.

It was best to keep quiet.

—

At first, I did my job wrong, and the complaints had merit.

I admit I messed up because I was busy helping customers.

That was wrong on so many levels. The customers were last on anyone's priority list.

They'd be shopping for an item and needed help, so I'd help them – obviously what customer service should be.

The problem was, I'd get in trouble for my area being a mess – like the products on the shelf wouldn't be lined up with military precision.

And every time it wasn't my fault – it'd be other irritating co-workers who I had to follow behind, who would mess up the store.

Inevitably, I just focused on cleaning the store and avoiding customers at all costs.

Anytime a customer came near, I would hide around the next aisle, so they wouldn't bother me, and I could get back to cleaning the store – and Corporate America wonders why some of these stores are going out of business? It's because of horrible training like that.

So, all day, every day, I'd go to work, organize shelves for 8 hours, and avoid customers and my boss.

Bizarrely, that was the path to success.

Our regional manager came to the store to grade us. He looked at my section of the store and marveled at how every row was packed tight and clean and all the products were displayed without gaps or holes.

They tracked me down later, to inform me of my heroic feat.

They wanted to know how I had done it, so I could spread my organizing ways to the rest of the store.

All I could say was, "I spend a lot of time there," with a smile.

How could I possibly explain I kept my section neat by avoiding both my boss and the customers? There was no way.

I had to keep quiet, and hopefully, they'd go away.

WORST GRADE

The worst grade I ever got was a 12. Like a 12/100. A 12%.

The embarrassing part was, I actually studied. I studied a lot.

Back in college, I had a challenging Biblical Studies class.

The class wasn't hard, or the professor challenging, but rather, it felt like I had never cracked open the Bible in my life.

Predestination? What's that. *Bema Seat?* Yeah, I got nothing.

It was like speaking a different language.

—

So, the quiz was composed of 20 multiple choice questions, worth a point each, and an essay worth 80 points.

The funny part is this: The essay was prepared ahead of time.

We knew the question and were able to study and prepare our answer. I studied, read the textbook and multiple external sources, and prepared a glowing essay. I had the entire thing written out beforehand, then committed the major bullet points to memory.

When the time came for the test, I hardly cared about those multiple choice questions – they wouldn't affect my final grade.

I figured, what's the worst that can happen? My essay is rock-solid. I'll easily cruise by with a B even if I tank every multiple choice question.

Nope. Not so fast.

Because I got a zero on the essay. And 12 correct on the multiple choice.

Thank goodness for the multiple choice. It would have been embarrassing to get a zero (cough).

—

The day our quizzes were handed back I was sick. I figured we weren't doing anything important and had already killed myself studying for the quiz. So I felt confident to take a day off.

Unfortunately, I ran into the professor in the café during lunch.

"You missed class today," he said, popping out of nowhere like a stalker.

"Sorry. I was sick," I apologized.

"Swing by my office this afternoon. I need to explain the grading."

"Oh."

That didn't sound good.

Professors never went out of their way to find you. But how bad could I have possibly done?

I aced that sucker, I knew it.

—

I found his office and visited during Open Office Hours.

"Have a seat," he said kindly, as the door swung shut.

I knew I was in trouble but didn't know why.

"Before I show you the grade, you need to know I'm offering retakes."

He handed me the quiz. 12. Circled in red ink.

Shoot. I was beyond confused.

He continued, "A handful of students are in the same boat as you. They didn't do well on the essay so I'm offering a second chance. I'm going to knock off some points, so the best you can do is an 80, but it's better than nothing."

Yeah, or better than a 12, I thought.

"I just wished you were in class today because it's not a big deal. I don't want that grade to be a reflection on your effort. Because your answer was actually fantastic. But you answered an entirely different question, which I found compelling. It would have been an A."

Um. Ok.

"Thanks?" I said as a question.

I wasn't sure if I should take the 12 and call it a day. Or put in all that studying and effort a second time.

I shrugged my shoulders and left.

—

I hung the quiz on my fridge, like an elementary school art project. Hanging there in all its pride. 12.

Everyone laughed.

They thought it was hysterical. Especially since I had worked so hard on the essay and needed to study all over again.

I retook the quiz and put in the same effort. I even took the time to reconfirm with the professor, asking, "Is this the right answer?" Before committing the information to memory a second time.

It was. And I passed.

Meanwhile, the 12 stayed on my fridge all semester.

A reminder of my folly. And a memento to taking the time, thinking, slowing down, and evaluating, before wasting countless hours on the wrong thing.

I never wanted to hear those words again: "You did a lot of work. But you're just wrong."

I'm never wrong. Sometimes I just don't know what the question was.

Besides, it's just not worth it. Even if you get a redo.

LEARNING

I had an employee with a learning disability.

As a manager, this was the toughest challenge I ever faced.

The trainer gave me a heads-up too, saying: "We're giving you Tyler. He had a hard time during training. But there's no one else here I'd trust him with."

Oh, geez. Thanks.

I'm not sure if that's a compliment to my training ability or my high-tolerance level for patience. Maybe both.

Or maybe I'm too stubborn to quit.

—

I met Tyler and liked him right away. He was a handsome dude. He was funny and had a lot going for him.

From first impressions, you wouldn't think there was anything wrong with this guy – just the opposite. He could probably be the CEO of a trendy internet startup company, and you wouldn't question his intelligence.

But the second we sat down and began role-playing telephone calls, I knew something was wrong.

—

"Ok, the first step is to answer the phone, introduce yourself, and thank them for calling," I explained. "So you'd say, 'Thank you for calling the Southern Investment Group. This is Tyler. How can I help you?' Can you do that?"

"Yes," he said.

"Ok, then say it back to me."

"I can't."

"Why?"

"I don't know what you said."

"It's the Southern Investment Group," I said again. "Say that back to me: Southern Investment Group."

"Ummmm," was his reply.

"Let's try it one word at a time, Southern.

"Southern," he mumbled.

"Investment."

"Investment," he struggled.

"Group."

"Group," he said finally.

"Great. Say it all together, Southern Investment Group," I said with high hopes for his achievement.

"Ummmm. I can't."

Crap. I had never seen this in my entire life. I didn't know what to do.

—

I spent an hour with Tyler, going over very basic details, and getting nowhere.

Answering the phone was the easy part. Everything after that was so much harder.

We had financial and legal questions to answer. He couldn't just say whatever he wanted. We had scripts and very difficult material to master.

How was he going to successfully navigate a customer question, if he couldn't even answer the phone properly?

At first, I gave him the benefit of the doubt. I figured he was nervous. And I was in his face for an hour, drilling him with questions.

But I gave him way more handholding than anyone else. None of my other reps had that level of handholding.

He simply didn't understand.

—

Tyler sat with one of my better reps, to shadow, and hopefully pick things up.

They got along well too. I saw them cracking jokes and having fun.

But I checked on them later and asked privately, "How'd Tyler do?"

"He's a moron, boss," my employee said. "He's got to go."

That's what I feared. I never like firing anyone, ever. I like to give everyone the benefit of the doubt and give them every opportunity to succeed. And I especially didn't want it to be my fault they left.

If they quit because of their own reasons, fine. But I wanted to have done everything in my power to help them thrive.

—

Ultimately, that decision was taken out of my hands.

My manager said, "Corporate wants you to grade all your reps. Old school letter grades. A to F. Be honest. They're never going to see the grade. It's for corporate only."

That sounded like a horrible trick. I knew the skill level of all my reps, who the A, B, and C employees were.

But the trouble was Tyler. He was brand new. Only starting that day.

"How should I grade Tyler?" I asked my boss.

"I don't care if he's new or not. Grade him on his potential if you have to."

I was sure Tyler was an F. He was certainly doing poorly. But the kid had just started. If after a week or two of training, and he still didn't get it, then fine, he'll get the grade he deserves.

But at the moment he was trying his best. And he was nice. I liked him.

I gave him a D.

—

The following morning, lots of people were missing.

That night, corporate had called every employee receiving a C or lower and asked them not to return to work the next day.

It was a culling – a cut of the weak.

Only the strong survived.

I felt horrible for everyone I graded a C. I wished I graded them higher, had I known what this was all about.

And for Tyler too, he was gone.

I had sunk hours into this kid, trying to get him up to speed, to get him in a respectable place, where he'd at least enjoy the job and be able to keep it.

But I never expected to see him fired. Not in his first week of work.

What a travesty.

And I'm sure it was the same story Tyler had heard his entire life. That he wasn't good enough, or smart enough. That he was dumb.

But I wonder if anyone had devoted enough time to him, told him that he could do it, and that he was in fact smart enough.

But I guess we'll never know. Because we gave up on him. Just like everyone else.

NOT QUITTING

An employee told me he was quitting.

"Here's my badge," he said. "I'm quitting."

"You're not quitting," I shot back.

"I have to," he said. "I have my baby at home and I can't stand being here. I need to leave."

"I know," I said. "That's exactly why you can't quit. What else are you going to do? You need this job. Sit back down."

He did. He got back to work.

—

He desperately needed the job. He needed the money.

Every day he'd complain about money, and being broke.

So when he announced he was quitting, I didn't understand the logic.

I talked to him privately after. I told him about failure, and what it means to stick through difficult times. I told him about some of my experiences.

I liked him. I didn't want him to leave.

And for me, as a manager, I had invested too many hours into him. He was an A-level employee. If he left, I'd need to replace him, and I'd probably get someone less qualified.

He had every reason to stay.

And I needed him just as much.

—

At lunch, I found his security badge in the breakroom.

He left it there. Walked out the door. And quit.

I didn't understand.

My entire life I had been taught to not quit things. If I sign up for something, I'm going to do it to the best of my ability, and then once I succeed or failed, at the end of the season I'll reassess and try again, or pursue the next thing.

But quitting? No. There's no such thing.

—

I realized how hard I made it for him. He didn't even say good-bye.

He had wanted to, initially. But all I gave him was grief.

He didn't want to hear my nonsense. So he walked out the door.

I learned a lot from that experience.

There are seasons for change, and not everything will work how I want to.

And sometimes I will put a lot of energy into people, but it doesn't mean they can't move on.

And it doesn't mean everyone thinks like me or has the same motivations as me.

After that, any time someone quit, I thanked them politely and wished them the best.

I didn't give them a hard time anymore. Because lots of people quit lots of things.

And if they've already decided in their mind they've "quit," there's nothing I can do to convince them otherwise.

So I let them go, peacefully, and with a smile on my face, thanking them for the good times we had together and for the effort they put forth.

Because at the end of the day, nothing lasts forever. We're all pursuing the next thing.

So in the meantime, why can't we all just get along?

COOKIE

My Grandma made the best chocolate chip cookies in the world.

Like, seriously.

You may think you've had a good cookie, but you really haven't. Maybe you've been to Paris or visited a celebrity chef bakery. But all of those are imitations and forgery.

Because the best cookies are at Grammy's house.

—

We'd visit occasionally – for holiday gatherings or birthday celebrations.

And inevitably, there'd be cookies. Always cookies.

There's a real estate joke that you should bake cookies before a prospective buyer arrives. And for good reason. Nothing smells more wholesome than fresh baked cookies.

And to me, nothing smells more like Grammy's house than a warm, gooey, chocolate chip cookie, piping hot from the oven.

I swear she timed her baking too, to finish at the exact moment we'd arrive.

We'd enter the house, say hi, and be greeted with a fresh plate of mouth-watering chocolate goodies, sliding right out of the oven.

Oh, man – those cookies were good.

I'd grab one off the rack, I didn't care how hot they were. And then I'd try and steal a second one, and run into the living room before my parents could remind me to have "only one."

How can you possibly eat only one cookie? You can't. It's impossible. Not when they're that delicious. It's too tempting.

If I could bottle that recipe, and jam it on a food truck, I'd have a rolling cash-making machine for all those cookie addicted folks. They'd follow me everywhere. Like the pied-piper of cookies.

I'd be a millionaire.

—

I asked my mom, "Why can't you make cookies like Grammy?"

I'm sure I touched a nerve, irritating her mother-ness to the core.

My mom made excellent food, and her desserts were always spectacular, but the chocolate chip cookies just weren't the same.

"I can't," Mom explained. "It's her oven."

Convenient excuse. As an 8-year-old boy, all I ever heard were excuses.

I wanted more of those cookies. And I wanted them at my house, to come piping hot out of my own kitchen, like a cookie ATM. On Demand Cookies.

Then I could eat them every day.

—

Then, horribly, the worst day of my adolescence arrived.

My grandparents got a kitchen makeover.

NOOOOOOOOOOOOOOOOO!!!!!!!!!!!

We arrived with great fanfare, to see the finished product and coveted upgrade to their house. Because really, in our "keep up with the Joneses" mentality, who doesn't want a fresh new kitchen?

Granite countertops? Check. Custom cabinets? Check. Stainless steel appliances? Double check.

And as we entered the party, celebrating their new material achievement, Grammy welcomed us with a fresh batch of her delicious cookies.

And even though the house looked different, sparkling and new – at least the pomp-and-circumstance of the cookie tradition remained.

The smell of fresh baked cookies welcomed us in, but something was different. The smell was different. It no longer smelled like Grammy's house.

And worse, the cookies no longer tasted the same.

I grabbed a cookie with hopeful resolve – wishing and hoping my childhood memories remained intact.

But no, there was something wrong. The cookie wasn't right.

And it wasn't that the cookies were bad – they were fine. But that was exactly the problem – they were just fine.

Gone was the epic flavor and assault on your sugary senses. Gone was the sweet buttery sensation you'd suck through your nose. And gone was the gooey texture of the world's best cookie.

No, instead, these were normal cookies – pedestrian food at best.

—

That day, I felt like someone had died.

When I should have been happy for my grandparents, and all their new shiny appliances, I wasn't. I was distraught. I was upset. And I was in a lot of pain.

On the car ride back, I asked, "What happened to Grammy's cookies? They're different," I asked.

My mom kept her gaze on the road ahead, looking aimlessly at the passing trees, resting on her chin – lost in thought, thinking, pondering.

"It's her oven," she explained sadly.

But maybe, she too was thinking about those cookies. And how she'd never get one again.

A recipe, a flavor, a taste – a memory – that would be lost forever.

BAD WORD

I learned a bad word.

On the bus, everyone was signing a fun new song.

Unfortunately, that song involved a very bad word – at least bad enough that a 10-year-old shouldn't know it.

And for the sake of my younger audience, let's pretend the word was "Liechtenstein."

—

"Liechtenstein, Liechtenstein, la-la-la Liechtenstein," we sang, over and over again.

It was a very fun song with a very catchy beat.

Though, none of us knew exactly what we were singing about – the word itself was so silly and none of us had heard it before – but one thing was certain, we weren't singing about a tiny central European country.

—

We were on a school camping trip – boys only – and this was our anthem for the weekend.

I don't know where the girls went. They had tea-time or something boring. But who cares about the girls, right – "boys rule!"

We marched through the woods, carrying our packs, food, and sleeping bags, singing our little song like the marching orders of the Seven Dwarfs – "Hi-ho, hi-ho."

We dropped our gear at the giant cabin and picked our beds for the night. When you're 10, everywhere feels awesome and new. And this cabin felt like a new exciting adventure, something to explore.

I felt full of energy like I had eaten too many Skittles and buzzed around on a sugar-high.

And most of all, that song played over and over in my head.

—

"Liechtenstein!" I shouted as I jumped off the front steps. I did a cool jump-spin, like I was a ninja out in the woods, and landed at the feet of my friends.

Ha! I was so cool. And this trip was going to be epic.

Except, our teacher had a different motive.

"All of you! Come here now!" He screamed.

Geez, man. What a buzz-kill. Why do adults always have a stick up their butt? This camping trip was supposed to be epic, exploring the woods, killing insects, making s'mores, and now it felt like the same drudgery of school.

Ugh. Kill me now. What do you want?

We stood in a circle, ashamed – like puppies with tails between their legs. We didn't know what we had done, but obviously, we were 10-year-old boys, and when weren't we in trouble?

"I'm very disappointed in you all," he said. "This was supposed to be a fun weekend. We need to make sure there's no name-calling, and we're all getting along. Alright?"

"Yes, sir," we agreed grumbling.

Adults do this thing where they collectively get the entire group in trouble, instead of singling out an individual. It's strange and unfair – it's also very confusing – what lesson are we supposed to be learning here?

"Now go play, and treat each other with respect. I expect more from you," he finished.

We scattered, off to collect branches, to use as swords – so we could stab each other.

"What was that about?" My friend asked.

"I have no idea," I said and went about my merry way. I shrugged my shoulder and stabbed my friend in the gut with a dull sword.

Because obviously, I hadn't done anything wrong.

—

It took me 20 years to figure out what happened that day.

Did I say "Liechtenstein" as I jumped off the stairs?

Oh, man. That's bad.

But it's also very very funny.

For one, I apologize to the teacher I offended. Clearly, I had no idea what word choice I had used.

Secondly, calling a group of boys a "Liechtenstein" makes absolutely no sense.

I can only imagine the horror running through my teacher's mind, hearing that word spoken on a boy's camping trip, and wondering how he'd squash the situation.

There'd be absolutely no way he'd explain the word. Just that it was bad. And shouldn't be uttered from the lips of a precious little boy.

At the very least, that was the end of the song. Our song of the summer had been extinguished.

Well, it was fun while it lasted.

"Liechtenstein!"

ABOUT THE AUTHOR

Joe Shaughnessy is a science fiction and fantasy author. His novels include *Orion's War* and *Lilly and the Forbidden Forest*. His short stories have appeared in *The Fable Online*, *Bewildering Stories*, and *Story Shack Magazine*. In *Escape the Cubicle*, Joe details his personal adventure of overcoming fear and being brave. Born and raised in New Hampshire, he currently lives in Florida with his wife.

To view upcoming projects, please connect with the author at www.joeshaughnessy.com. If you'd like more stories by Joe, please follow him on Patreon, at www.patreon.com/joeshaughnessy.

www.ingramcontent.com/pod-product-compliance
Lightning Source LLC
Chambersburg PA
CBHW021812170526
45157CB00007B/2553